The Secret Superpower of High Functioning Leaders

How Process Intelligence (PQ) Creates
Unstoppable Teams and Unbeatable Results

by

SHANE YOUNT & ROB KORNBLUM

THE OAKLEA PRESS

WWW.OAKLEAPRESS.COM

Praise for Process Intelligence (PQ)
& Competitive Solutions, Inc.

"I've had the privilege of knowing the CSI team for over 15 years, and from the very first day of training, I was hooked. Shane and his colleagues have been exceptional mentors to me throughout my career, offering guidance that's shaped how I approach leadership at different companies given the challenges. The methodologies, behaviors, and leadership techniques he and his team taught me have been invaluable. I apply these principles every day in my standard work, and Process Based Leadership® has become my go-to approach for guiding my teams toward achieving company goals. I live by the three C's: clarity, consistency, and connectivity, which has led to my teams' continued success. I'm deeply grateful for the opportunity to learn and grow with these powerful methodologies.

—Snehal Patel,
Chief Technical Officer

Sana
Biotechnology

"I was first introduced to Shane and the CSI team along with their management/performance review methodologies while working in a manufacturing plant that was not performing on many fronts. Shane and the CSI team taught us the importance of defining our "winning and losing" metrics and the criticality of ensuring that EVERYONE in the organization, from the shop floor to the site leadership team, were kept informed of our winning or losing status. Shane stressed the art and importance of Gemba - going to where the work happens, asking questions, and coaching - and the importance of a bidirectional escalation process. He taught us discipline (standing meetings where you stand for the entire meeting!!!) and the critical "team contract." There is something about seeing in print the agreements you make, the behaviors you will abide by, the governance process you will use - and then signing your name to it. That codifies the leadership team's ways of working, driving team dynamics and performance to a new level.

"As I have progressed through my career, each role being more senior in nature, I have shared the Process Based Leadership® methodologies with my leadership teams to ensure we ground ourselves as a team. It takes work and continuous assessment of performance to transform good teams into great teams. And I can honestly say as I look back, the team I was leading when I first learned these methodologies turned out to be one of the best performing I have ever experienced. Hard work pays off!"

Lynn A Bottone,
VP Biotech Operations,

Pfizer

"As a participant in the Army's Organic Industrial Base Leadership Course, customer to CSI's Process Based Leadership®, and a personal mentee, the relationship with Shane and the CSI team is forged through a shared vision, aligned thinking, and doing what is right for both the business and our people. CSI's processes and methodologies have brought my organization of more than 600 people and operating revenue of $400M to new heights. CSI has taught us how to move from transactional operations to generational transformation. That mindset has shaped how we lead, how we adapt, and how we grow—turning complexity into opportunity and fostering resilience at every level of the business. We have driven the business forward financially, modernized our systems and infrastructure, and developed our workforce by leaps and bounds since we partnered with the CSI Team. Shane is a transformational leader and radiates those qualities in all his interactions. We are forever indebted to him for his leadership."

—Anthony Fabrizio
Deputy Commander

"Having had the privilege of working closely with Shane and the CSI Team over the past decade, I can attest to the transformative impact his insights on leadership have had on my personal journey. Shane's thought processes and methodologies are a masterclass in setting clear goals, engaging and developing people, and implementing systems for repeatable excellence. His approach to building a high-performing leadership culture, centered on the pillars of clarity, connectivity, and consistency, is both practical and inspiring, and it has become my mantra. Shane's guidance has not only refined my leadership style but has also fundamentally improved my team's performance and elevated our business results."

—Dr. Rebecca Teeters,
President, 3M Chemical Operations LLC

"The enduring power of CSI's mantra—consistency and clarity—has enabled colleagues at all levels of my organization to become truly aligned and connected. Over the years, Shane and the CSI Team has imparted some of the most valuable leadership and life lessons I've ever received, centered on the delicate balance between accountability and personal empathy. Ironically, while Shane consistently drives teams to focus on their operating metrics, the true impact he has had in transforming these teams and organizations is immeasurable. From the very first leadership project kick-off meeting to the ongoing daily shift huddles, CSI's systems serve as a powerful performance multiplier. Beyond being a highly trusted thought partner, Shane is, most importantly, a genuine friend."

—Edward DuBeau,
SVP & Global Business Lead
NextGen ERP Program
zoetis

"Over the past 20 years leading diverse teams, I've found few frameworks as impactful as Process Based Leadership®—the system developed by my friend and longtime colleague, Shane Yount and the amazing team at Competitive Solutions. Their work has not only guided me as a leader but has empowered the teams I've served to build cultures rooted in accountability, clarity, and continuous improvement. Their insights offer both new and seasoned leaders a practical, proven path to drive productivity and foster ownership at every level. Having worked alongside Shane and the CSI team through the years, I've seen firsthand the power of their approach, and I continue to be inspired by their leadership

I only wish I had discovered their work earlier in my career—it would have made a world of difference."

—Matt Pearson
Vice President,
Quality System & Risk Management

GUARDANT

"Our shared commitment to Process Based Leadership® has profoundly shaped not only my personal growth but also the trajectory of the organizations I've led. It goes far beyond the mechanics of a scorecard-it's about the intentionality behind measuring what truly matters. The discipline embedded in our methodologies-anchored in ownership, accountability, clarity, consistency, and connectedness – has instilled a mindset that elevates leadership from reactive management to proactive transformation. This approach has unified leadership teams, fostered a culture of trust and alignment, and driven plant performance to unprecedented levels. It's not just a framework, it's a philosophy that turns metrics into meaning and processes into purpose."

—Michelle Dixon,
Vice President of MTO, VC

Alcon
SEE BRILLIANTLY

"CSI's leadership philosophy and "Process Based" methodologies have been instrumental in shaping how I approach organizational performance and growth. Shane and the team's emphasis on "Process Intelligence" has repeatedly proven to be a competitive advantage—

turning strategy into measurable results and aligning teams around a clear, repeatable framework for success. Through CSI's inspriational message, I've seen how disciplined processes drive operational excellence and create a culture of accountability and continuous improvement. Shane and team have left a lasting impact on the organizations I've led, and your work continues to stand as a benchmark for effective, sustainable leadership in today's complex business environment. I am thankful for our initial connection, and the efficacy of your program drives my desire to bring these methodologies to every business endeavor I am involved with."

—Kyle Hogan,

Chief Operating Officer

PORT**CORPUS CHRISTI**

"I met Shane and the CSI team at a point in my career when I wasn't sure I had the ability to scale Phenix beyond the limits I had already reached. His Process Based Leadership® model and tools gave me more than a framework, they gave me confidence, clarity, and a completely new way of leading. By focusing on real-time business metrics, we began to understand if we were truly winning or losing each day. That shift in thinking encouraged open communication, increased accountability across the organization, and created a culture of trust where people understood both their role and their impact. Shane and the CSI team helped me learn that true transformation isn't about "fixing culture" but about putting the right processes in place and the culture evolves as a result.

"In my 38 years of leading Phenix Label, nothing has been more impactful than the sustainable systems and processes we developed with Shane and CSI. The consistency of his methodology allowed us to replicate excellence, address problems so they were never repeated, and build a foundation where accountability and engagement became the norm. Today, we continue to use those tools to prosper and sustain our competitive advantage, and I am now passing them on to my son Charlie as he prepares to lead Phenix into its fifth generation as a family-owned business. Shane and CSI didn't just help us hit goals in the short term, they gave us the processes to transform how we lead and ensure that our success carries on well into the future."

—Hans Peter
President & CEO

PHENIX

"From our earliest meeting, my professional relationship with Shane Yount and Competitive Solutions, Inc (CSI) has been a model of trust, respect, and shared purpose. Their approach to business leadership has not only catalyzed remarkable transformation within the organizations I have led but has also profoundly influenced my own outlook as a leader. By introducing us to methodologies that prioritize transparency, continuous improvement, and robust engagement at every level, they have enabled us to cultivate environments where accountability is not just a word, but a lived value. This shift has been transformative. Our teams, once plagued by uncertainty over goals and expectations, are now unified by clear metrics, shared priorities, and a collective sense of ownership. The ripple effects of this clarity have extended far beyond improved performance indicators—they have fostered a culture of mutual respect, candor, and relentless pursuit of excellence. Over the years, I have come to regard our partnership as a source of inspiration and a benchmark for excellence in organizational effectiveness. I can say with complete confidence that our relationship with Competitive Solutions has been among the most positive, productive, and rewarding of my career. Their practical methodologies have not only delivered concrete results but have also left an indelible mark on the way I lead and the cultures I strive to cultivate."

—Frank R. Hacker,
Vice President - Manufacturing
rockline
people who make it right

(S) Competitive Solutions Inc.

"Optimizing People, Processes, & Performance"

Competitive Solutions, Inc. (CSI) is a recognized leader in organizational transformation, helping companies in performance-driven industries build sustainable cultures of clarity, connectivity, and consistency. With a proven consulting methodology (Process Based Leadership®), business execution software solutions (Visuant®), and custom leadership coaching programs (Leadership GPS®), CSI equips clients to dramatically improve bottom-line business results.

For over three decades, CSI has delivered measurable impact for clients such as 3M, Alcon, US Army, Pfizer, Harley-Davidson, Rockline Industries, and many others. The firm is known for its agility, adapting quickly, tailoring its approach, and delivering practical solutions that fit the needs of each client. By helping clients to develop leadership systems that outlast personalities, CSI enables organizations to improve accountability, ownership, and clarity into the very fabric of their companies.

At the heart of CSI's approach is a belief in purpose-driven impact. Every CSI engagement is fueled by a commitment to help leaders become the best versions of themselves, fostering alignment, and creating environments where people thrive. That genuine care for both clients and colleagues is what transforms projects into long-term partnerships and measurable improvements into lasting legacies.

Today, under the leadership of CEO Rob Kornblum and Chairman Shane Yount, CSI continues its mission of optimizing people, processes, and performance. As CSI moves forward, its impact endures – one leader, one team, one organization at a time.

Process Based Leadership® VISUANT™
Visual • Accountable • Results

LEADERSHIP™ GPS

Over the last 35 years, CSI has worked with organizations such as Colgate-Palmolive, Genentech, The US Army, 3M, Revlon, Rockline, Alcon, Roche, and hundreds of other organizations to achieve just a few of the following business results:

SAFETY
53% Recordable injury Reduction

SAFETY
90% Reduction in incidents over a 3-year period

COST
Favorable Manufacturing Variance of $3.8M

Delivery
Lowest back order levels in 10 years

QUALITY
Right first time up 12% in six months

EFFICIENCY
98.7% reduction in Action Item Cycle Time

PEOPLE
Absenteeism reduced 13%

EFFICIENCY
Operating efficiencies improved more than 20% within first year

RELIABILITY
Unplanned downtime reduced by 25% in six months

3M

COLGATE PALMOLIVE

Alcon

RUST-OLEUM
INDUSTRIAL BRANDS

rockline
people who make it right

CONTENTS

Contents

ACKNOWLEDGMENTS

To the hundreds of companies we have visited and the thousands of leaders who have trusted us the past 35 years, we say, "Thank You!" It has been the honor of my life to be able to do this work. It hasn't been easy, it is often challenging and exhausting, but when you witness and experience true transformation both personally and organizationally, it all becomes worthwhile. We have seen front line supervisors who followed the tenets of this book and now hold positions in boardrooms and C-Suites. Believing there is a system stronger than one's personality, proximity, and powers of persuasion requires trust and fortitude. The headwinds created by legacy leadership theories are formidable, but if you are able to see beyond the traditional way many organizations have defined leadership and grasp the potential power of simple systems, your leadership mindset will change forever. It is our hope that as you read these chapters, you will see the power of PQ—Process Intelligence—and how it serves to teach leaders the most powerful leadership lesson to date. It's not about you, it's about the systems we build, support, and sustain that truly allow us to, "Leave a Leadership Legacy."

We are deeply grateful for those executives who offered their endorsements, words of encouragement, and for their trust in allowing Competitive Solutions, Inc. (CSI) to walk beside you all these years.

Hope you enjoy …

PREFACE

During more than 35 years in business as Competitive Solutions Inc. (CSI), we have met countless leaders from all over the world, some seasoned and experienced, others green and naïve. During that entire time, we have done our best to discover and to understand why some leaders thrive and others do not. We have always been curious to know why a few leave an indelible mark on their people and their organizations, how could some "Leave a Leadership Legacy," while others, after they have left the organization, appear never to have been there at all. Sadly, they are like a mist that fades and evaporates, leaving no trace whatsoever.

Leadership development is not a new concept. Those in charge of organizations have been trying to "fix" their leaders for as long as there have been people to lead. There are many, perhaps thousands of philosophies about which attributes come together to create a high-functioning leader. No shortage exists of models and Venn diagrams that articulate the characteristics, imperatives, or capabilities leaders should have in order to be successful.

Unfortunately, that is where it often ends—with a list of "desired" traits that frame effective leadership. Adjectives, if you will, that describe good leadership. So, those in charge take these adjectives and try to assess and evaluate their leaders against them. On the surface, that seems fine. But this approach is one-dimensional. It describes the attributes to identify a future high-functioning leader, but it leaves out an important component, in fact, what this book will suggest is most important—which is to create harmony with a personality-driven management style and then combine it with system-driven leadership.

How are you or we as leaders supposed to become high-functioning? Are we to simply aspire and then evaluate ourselves every quarter to see if we are getting closer to or farther away from exhibiting those attributes? Certainly, self-reflection is important, but is that going to be all we need to do? Maybe we should find a mentor and have that person help us with our "blind spots." It's true that having an accountability partner or mentor to provide unfiltered feedback and suggestions on how to improve is a key component of leadership. In addition, maybe we need to undergo more training and read more books. Education will surely help us become better versions of our leadership selves.

The Crisis in Leadership Today

We are facing an unprecedented leadership crisis that traditional development approaches cannot solve. Recent data from Gallup reveals the stark reality: only 21% of employees are engaged at work, and perhaps even more alarming, only 27% of managers, those responsible for leading others, report being engaged in their roles. Think about that for a moment. Less than one in three of the people charged with leading our organizations are truly committed to their work, or are connected to it.

This engagement crisis has real consequences. Leadership fatigue has reached epidemic proportions. In a recent survey we conducted among executives, 78% reported feeling "overwhelmed" or "burned out" by the constant demands of their roles. The COVID-19 pandemic accelerated this trend, forcing leaders to navigate unimaginable scenarios without preparation or support.

Simultaneously, the workforce is experiencing a dramatic demographic shift as Baby Boomers exit the workforce at a rate of approximately 10,000 per day. This exodus represents an enormous loss of institutional knowledge and leadership experience that few organizations are prepared to address.

These forces are converging to create what we call the "leadership sustainability crisis," a perfect storm that will increasingly divide organizations into those that thrive and those that merely survive or ultimately fail.

Beyond IQ and EQ: The Missing Link in Leadership

Many traditional leadership development strategies speak to the IQ of leaders, which begs the questions: How can we get feedback, get smarter, become more self-aware, more knowledgeable? IQ is absolutely a key component of successful leadership. We often lean on our HR and recruiting partners to help us find the "best" candidates who have the most experience, education, and high-quality credentials. We all want to work with smart people. Nevertheless, IQ alone isn't the superpower.

Much has been written and said in the last 20 years about EQ, or Emotional Intelligence, as a key driver of high-functioning leaders. We can't say enough about the power of EQ. The ability to listen, to engage, to question, to demonstrate curiosity, be teachable, and show up are essential leadership attributes. Every leader should have a "lifelong learning goal" to master and exhibit the elements of EQ. A senior executive recently shared the following message with his team: "Not all readers are leaders, but ALL leaders are readers." Seeking to better understand oneself and to improve how we engage with those around us is a noble and honorable endeavor.

Our experience indicates that this is where most leadership development ends: smart people (IQ) are hired and taught soft skills (EQ). That should be enough, right?

Wrong.

What is the "Superpower" of high-functioning leaders?

After so many years of observing, doing, and learning, we believe there is a critical third dimension that has been largely unexplored in leadership development. This missing element, what we call the third leg of the leadership stool, is what gives high-functioning leaders their true superpower. It's what enables them to create organizations that thrive not because of their constant presence and intervention, but because of the systems and processes they put in place.

This third dimension focuses on scalability and sustainability. It shifts leadership from being personality-dependent to being process-driven. It's what allows great leaders to leave a lasting legacy—organizations that continue to excel long after they've moved on.

The third dimension is Process Intelligence, or PQ. PQ is what makes a lasting, durable, and authentic legacy. PQ binds an organization together around the power of systems and processes—rather than personalities.

In our travels across industries and around the globe, we've witnessed firsthand the dramatic difference between organizations that rely on exceptional individuals versus those that build exceptional systems. The former are regularly vulnerable, one retirement, one regulation, one extended absence can throw operations into disarray. The latter demonstrates remarkable resilience, maintaining performance even through significant leadership transitions.

The Journey Ahead: What This Book Offers

In the chapters that follow, we'll explore PQ, this missing third dimension of leadership and how it works together with IQ and EQ to create truly high-functioning leadership. We'll examine how organizations historically have overemphasized IQ in hiring and promotion decisions, the evolution toward recognizing the importance of EQ, and how PQ can complete the picture for those organizations that embody it.

This book is not about quick fixes or trendy leadership theories. It's about building fundamental capabilities that allow organizations to perform consistently at high levels regardless of who holds any particular position. It's about creating leadership that leaves a lasting legacy rather than simply creating a temporary fix.

Whether you are a seasoned executive, a frontline supervisor, or someone aspiring to leadership, the principles in this book offer a pathway to greater impact, reduced stress, and truly sustainable success.

Let's begin the journey together.

Shane Yount & Rob Kornblum

Chapter One

What Makes a High-Functioning Leader?

In the rapidly evolving landscape of modern business, the definition of effective leadership is undergoing a significant transformation. The traditional model, which has long relied on a combination of high intelligence quotient (IQ) and emotional intelligence (EQ), is proving insufficient to meet the complex challenges of today's corporate world. This chapter introduces a groundbreaking third dimension of leadership: Process Intelligence (PQ), which represents the missing link in creating leaders capable of building sustainable, scalable, and high-performing organizations.

One of the key signs of a high functioning team and organization is the ability of team members to answer what seems like a simple question: "Are we winning or losing? (today, this week, this month, this quarter). People want to be part of a winning team, and they generally want to fix what is broken. It's a key question that CSI asks our clients, and the members of those teams, when we start an engagement. Not being able to answer that question is certainly an element of the abysmally low employee engagement issue that we highlighted in the Preface. Companies that demonstrate leadership excellence often have a few important traits that we will showcase throughout the book: ready access to the right metrics, a process for reviewing that data regularly, an action plan to take corrective actions, a communication model to work through difficult issues, and a culture of accountability without blame.

A Tale of Two Leaders

Consider the case of Sarah, a CEO known for her hands-on approach to leadership. Every day, she arrived at the office ready to tackle any challenge that came her way. Her employees often joked that she wore an invisible red cape and was always prepared to swoop in and save the day. Sarah prided herself on her ability to solve problems quickly and efficiently. She was involved in every decision, from major strategic moves to the minutiae of daily operations. Her team marveled at her energy and dedication, but they also grew increasingly dependent on her constant presence.

The true test of Sarah's leadership came when she finally took a long-overdue vacation. In her absence, the company's operations began to falter. Simple decisions were delayed, waiting for her input. Projects stalled without her oversight. By the end of the week, it became clear that while Sarah was an exceptional problem solver, she had inadvertently created an organization that couldn't function without her.

This scenario illustrates a common pitfall: the creation of a personality-dependent organization rather than a process-driven one. While Sarah's high IQ and EQ made her an effective crisis manager, her approach didn't allow for the development of robust systems and processes that could operate in her absence.

Now contrast this with another leader I observed—a plant manager who had led his facility for fifteen years and was approaching retirement. There was no panic, no desperate knowledge transfer sessions in his final months. Why? Because this leader had built robust systems: clear scorecards, structured meeting processes, standardized problem-solving approaches, and documented expectations. He had created processes that functioned extremely well and would continue to function well regardless of who occupied the corner office.

This comparison underscores the critical importance of what I call Process Intelligence (PQ) in modern leadership. While the ability to "save the day" might seem admirable, true leadership excellence lies in creating an organization that rarely needs saving in the first place.

Introducing Process Intelligence (PQ): The Third Leg of Leadership

Process Intelligence (PQ) represents the systematic capability to design, implement, and orchestrate processes that deliver consistent, scalable results. While IQ addresses cognitive abilities and EQ focuses on interpersonal skills, PQ concentrates on building the organizational backbone that enables sustainable performance.

PQ is what makes a lasting, durable, and authentic legacy. It binds an organization together around the power of systems and processes, rather than personalities. PQ becomes the "run the business" methodology, allowing leaders to move up, move on, and move out without missing a beat. It is the foundation of sustainability and the key to "leaving a leadership legacy."

As James Clear, the author of the bestselling book *Atomic Habits* states, "You do not rise to the level of your goals, you sink to the level of your systems."

The Traditional Leadership Model: IQ and EQ

For decades, businesses have focused on two primary factors when selecting and developing leaders:

IQ: The Entry Ticket

Intelligence Quotient, or IQ, has traditionally been viewed as the price of admission to leadership roles. Organizations seek individuals with sharp analytical skills, quick problem-solving abilities, and a capacity for complex thinking. These cognitive abilities are undeniably crucial in navigating the challenges of modern business.

However, an overreliance on IQ creates several problems. It often leads to the promotion of the most skilled individual contributors into leadership roles—a practice that can be problematic. As we often observe in organizations, "You're the best technician, you're the best engineer, you're the best salesperson. Why don't you become a supervisor or team leader?" This approach, while seemingly logical, often overlooks the distinct skill set required for effective leadership.

The skills that made someone a great individual contributor are no longer the skills they need most as a leader. Promoting a software engineer to team lead means they now have to deal with budgets, paperwork, people development, and communication issues that require them to rely on skills they may not have, as well as to perform tasks they find difficult or unpleasant.

EQ: The People Factor

Recognizing the limitations of an IQ-centric approach, organizations began to emphasize emotional intelligence (EQ). This shift acknowledged that effective leadership extends beyond cognitive capabilities to include inter-personal skills and emotional awareness.

Most corporate "leadership training" tends to focus on EQ: intentional communication, active listening, demonstrating empathy, managing change effectively, executive "presence," and much more. Leaders with high EQ are often charismatic, empathetic, and skilled at building relationships. The focus on EQ has undoubtedly improved leadership in many organizations, resulting in more engaged teams and better workplace dynamics.

However, while EQ is a crucial component of leadership, it is not a complete solution. The combination of IQ and EQ, while powerful, nevertheless leaves a critical gap in the skill set needed for truly high-functioning leadership in today's complex business environment.

The Unintended Consequences of the IQ-EQ Model

The prevalence of the IQ-EQ leadership model has led to several unintended consequences that are becoming increasingly problematic:

1. Leadership Fatigue: Leaders who rely heavily on their IQ and EQ often find themselves in a constant state of personally solving problems, which leads to burnout. As one executive recently told me, "There's tremendous leadership fatigue in our industry today. We're all feeling worn out and used up. The pandemic pushed us to our limits—we can't sustain that tempo indefinitely."

The Gallup data we mentioned earlier demonstrates the extent of this fatigue, with only 27% of managers considered "engaged." Twenty-seven percent—only about one in four! How many of those managers are looking for new roles elsewhere? How well do you think their teams are performing?

2. Scalability Issues: As organizations grow, leadership based primarily on individual capabilities (IQ) and personal relationships (EQ) becomes difficult if not impossible to scale. Leaders cannot maintain the same level of personal involvement with every aspect of an expanding business.

Too often we see leaders who have been promoted still doing the job they left rather than the job they now have. Why does the previous job have this gravitational pull? Often it's because the individual had mastered that job. It was something they did really well, what set them apart and got them promoted. Unfortunately, that makes it hard to leave that job behind. It's why some leaders find themselves managing down rather than up, inserting themselves back into the old role.

3. Personality Dependency: A leadership style that emphasizes EQ without robust processes can create loyalty to individual personalities rather than to the organization itself. This becomes evident when a key person leaves and other high-potential employees follow, often citing the departed leader's influence as their primary motivation.

4. Inconsistent Performance: Without established systems and processes, performance can vary widely depending on which leader is in charge or how engaged they are at any given time.

5. Limited Leadership Pipeline: When promotion decisions are based primarily on IQ and EQ, organizations may overlook potential leaders who have a natural aptitude for creating and managing effective systems and processes.

Fenced in by the 3Ps' Leadership Circle Trap

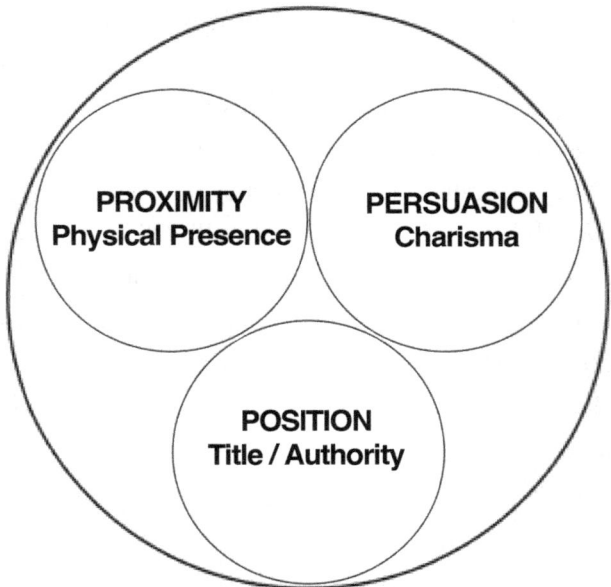

PROXIMITY
Physical Presence

PERSUASION
Charisma

POSITION
Title / Authority

These approaches create dependency and limit salability. Teams become reliant on the leader's presence, charisma, or authority.

Understanding the PQ Spectrum

To understand the impact of PQ, it's useful to examine the spectrum from low-functioning to high-functioning PQ:

Low-Functioning PQ

Organizations with low-functioning PQ exhibit several characteristic patterns:

Reactive Leadership: Leaders frequently find themselves caught in a cycle of firefighting, where the focus is predominantly on crisis management. They react to problems as they arise rather than preventing them, creating a culture where issues are only addressed in their advanced stages.

Inconsistent Processes: Different departments operate in isolation, each following their own unique approach. This lack of uniformity leads to inefficiencies, redundancy, and miscommunications that stifle productivity and slow project delivery.

Personality-Dependent Culture: The organization's successes are overly dependent on certain individuals whose personal relationships and knowledge are pivotal. This reliance becomes a critical weakness if a key player exits.

Lack of Accountability: Without clear processes, measuring performance becomes subjective and accountability becomes difficult to enforce. Employees can deflect failures by citing miscommunications or ambiguous instructions.

Short-Term Focus: Immersed in daily operational demands, leaders struggle with long-term strategic planning. Urgent problems consume time and resources, over-shadowing the necessity to work toward long-term goals.

High-Functioning PQ

In contrast, organizations with high-functioning PQ demonstrate:

Proactive Leadership: Leaders prioritize setting up systems that predict and prevent problems. Instead of merely reacting, they invest in understanding potential challenges and implement solutions preemptively.

Standardized Processes: Standardized processes across departments ensure consistent operations and facilitate seamless communication and coordination, allowing for smooth scaling regardless of organizational complexity or size.

System-Driven Culture: Success is driven by institutional knowledge and shared processes rather than individual personalities. This approach ensures continuity and resilience even when personnel changes occur.

Clear Accountability: With clear processes in place, tracking performance becomes systematic and roles become transparent. Organizations can link outcomes directly to individual or team contributions, fostering a culture of responsibility and trust.

Long-Term Planning: By freeing leaders from constant crisis management, robust processes allow leaders to focus on strategic visioning and planning, facilitating continuous improvement and adaptability.

The Four Components of Process Intelligence

This book will unpack and explore the four non-negotiable components of PQ:

1. **Business Acumen Process** - How to systematize intelligence throughout your organization by creating a "Thermostatic Meter Process."

2. **Execution Process** - Creating systematic execution process that drives visual and measurable engagement.

3. **Communication Process** - Creating a rhythm and cadence of information flow tht puts leaders on offense.

4. **Ideal Behavior Process** - Building sustainable excellence through process-driven expectations.

Each component works together to create the organizational backbone that enables consistent high performance regardless of individual presence or absence.

The Three Ps: The Pitfall of Personality-Driven Management

A common trap that many leaders with high IQ and EQ fall into is what we term the "Three P's": Proximity, Persuasion, and Position. These represent approaches to management that, while potentially effective in the short term, undermine long-term organizational health and scalability.

Proximity: This approach emphasizes the physical presence of a leader to drive performance. While this can momentarily boost performance, it fails to create sustained motivation. Once the leader steps away, teams typically revert to previous patterns.

Persuasion: Leaders rely on personal charm or influence to motivate and achieve results. This creates "selective

Process Intelligence Versus The Three P's Approach

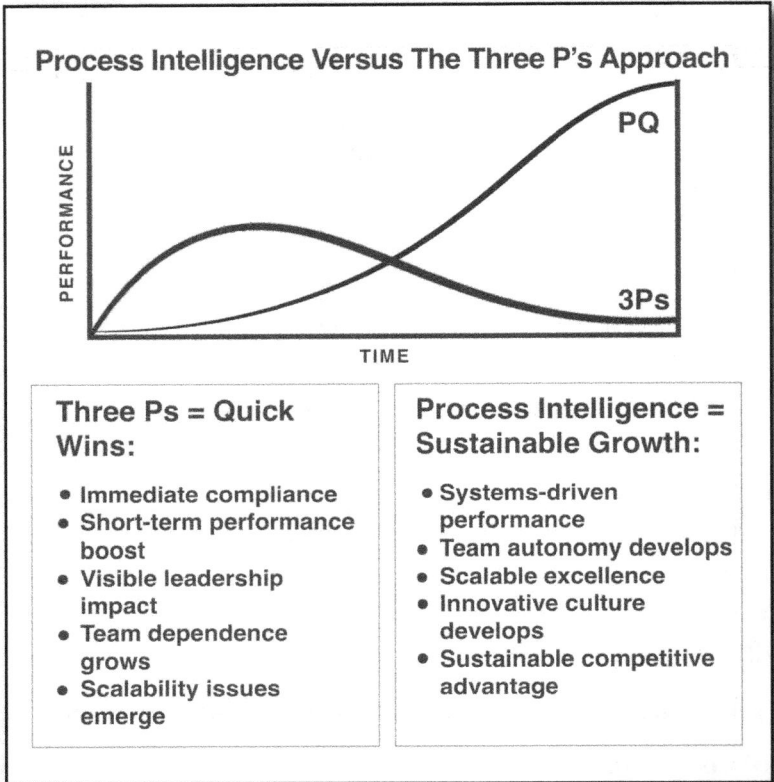

Three Ps = Quick Wins:	Process Intelligence = Sustainable Growth:
• Immediate compliance • Short-term performance boost • Visible leadership impact • Team dependence grows • Scalability issues emerge	• Systems-driven performance • Team autonomy develops • Scalable excellence • Innovative culture develops • Sustainable competitive advantage

engagement" and can breed dependency, where a team's effectiveness is contingent on personal interactions with the leader.

Position: Leveraging one's title or authority to drive results. This can yield immediate compliance but often fails to inspire genuine ownership or innovation, leading to a culture of mere compliance rather than proactive problem-solving.

The Power of Building Systems, Not Dependencies

The transition from personality-driven to PQ-focused leadership involves creating systems that function effectively regardless of specific individuals. This approach addresses the leadership sustainability crisis by building organizational capability that transcends any single person's talents or limitations. High-functioning PQ leaders focus on building systems that:

Clarify Expectations: Clear, well-defined metrics show roles and responsibilities, improving individual performance and fostering connection to organizational goals

Drive Accountability: Systems make account-ability process-driven rather than personality-driven, creating consistent standards regardless of individual leadership styles

Ensure Consistency: Processes maintain uniform performance levels across diverse teams, shifts, or locations

Enable Scalability: Robust processes facilitate swift onboarding and integration, allowing organizations to expand without sacrificing quality

Facilitate Continuous Improvement: Mechanisms for ongoing feedback and iterative development keep organizations dynamic and responsive to change

Conclusion: The Future of Leadership

As we progress through this book, we will explore how to develop and implement Process Intelligence as the critical third dimension of high-functioning leadership. The leaders of tomorrow cannot rely solely on being the most intelligent in the room or the most emotionally astute. While these qualities remain valuable, they must be accompanied by mastery of Process Intelligence.

The future belongs to leaders who can construct organizations that are resilient, adaptable, and capable of consistently maintaining high performance. The goal is not to create a system where leaders must constantly intervene to "save the day," but rather to build an organization where, due to robust, well-designed processes, such interventions are rarely necessary.

A leader's true legacy is not built on personal achievements or charisma, but on the systems and processes left behind. When a leader departs an organization, the measure of their impact lies in how well the organization continues to function in their absence.

We believe that a PQ-driven leadership model is a key to connecting strategy with execution. As Thomas Edison once said, "Vision without execution is hallucination."

The question for every aspiring high-functioning leader becomes: Are you building an organization that depends on your personal IQ and EQ, or are you creating a PQ-driven system that can excel without your constant presence? The answer to this question will determine whether you leave a lasting leadership legacy or simply fade away like mist when you move on.

This is echoed by what Michelle Dixon, Vice President of MTO, VC, Alcon said, "Our shared commitment to Process Based Leadership® has profoundly shaped not only my personal growth but also the trajectory of the organizations I've led. It goes far beyond the mechanics of a scorecard-it's about the intentionality behind measuring what truly matters. The discipline embedded in our methodologies-anchored in ownership, accountability, clarity, consistency, and connectedness – has instilled a mindset that elevates leadership from reactive management to proactive transformation. This approach has unified leadership teams, fostered a culture of trust and alignment, and driven plant performance to unprecedented levels. It's not just a framework, it's a philosophy that turns metrics into meaning and processes into purpose."

In the chapters that follow, we will explore practical strategies for developing Process Intelligence and creating organizations that thrive independently of any single individual. Prepare to have your preconceptions about effective leadership challenged as we explore this new paradigm that promises to revolutionize organizational performance and leadership effectiveness.

WORKBOOK

Leadership Self-Assessment: IQ, EQ, and PQ

Rate yourself on a scale of 1 (Strongly Disagree) to 5 (Strongly Agree) for each statement.

IQ (Intelligence Quotient)

I quickly analyze complex problems and identify key issues.
____

I use data and logic effectively to make decisions. ____

I easily explain complex concepts in simple terms. ____

IQ Score: ____ / 15

EQ (Emotional Intelligence)

I accurately identify my emotions and understand their impact. ____

I control impulsive feelings and adapt to changing circumstances. ____

I listen attentively and understand others' perspectives. ____

I inspire others and manage conflicts effectively. ____

EQ Score: ____ / 20

PQ (Process Intelligence)

I use data and metrics consistently to drive decision-making.
____

I establish and regularly update clear, repeatable processes.
____

I implement effective communication rhythms and accountability systems. ___

I document procedures and reduce dependency on individuals for key processes. ___

PQ Score: ___ / 20

Reflection

What are your strengths across IQ, EQ, and PQ?

Which area needs the most development?

What specific actions can you take to improve your weakest area?

How might enhancing all three dimensions make you a more effective leader?

Remember, this assessment is a starting point.

Chapter Two

We Hire for IQ – The Intelligence Trap

In the previous chapter, we explored how traditional leadership models have been built primarily on two dimensions: Intelligence Quotient (IQ) and Emotional Intelligence (EQ). IQ has long served as the gateway to leadership positions, i.e., those with sharp cognitive and analytical abilities. In contrast, EQ introduced crucial interpersonal capabilities, fostering leaders who could connect and communicate effectively with their teams. However, a critical element of leadership was missing in this framework: Process Intelligence (PQ).

We discovered that the traditional reliance on IQ and EQ often leads to unintended consequences. When sustaining performance depends heavily on their direct involvement, leaders can become fatigued from the relentless need for their personal intervention. In addition, organizations encounter scalability challenges as they grow, finding it difficult to maintain consistent processes across expanding teams. Moreover, there is an over-reliance on individual personalities, where team success becomes dependent on influential figures rather than robust systems, leading to inconsistent performance across different departments and teams.

Having recognized these pitfalls, we introduced PQ as a necessary third dimension of leadership—the ability to create, implement, and manage systems that drive consistent, scalable results. Leaders equipped with high-functioning PQ are able to design environments that are proactive rather than reactive, and they establish standardized processes that ensure reliability. They also cultivate system-dependent cultures rather than those reliant on individual personality traits. This enables clear accountability and facilitates long-term planning and improvement.

The previous chapter highlighted the importance of moving beyond the constraints of the "Three P's" — Proximity, Persuasion, and Position. It underscored the need to build organizations capable of thriving independently of any single individual's constant oversight.

In Chapter Two, we will examine how an enduring focus on IQ when making hiring and promotion decisions has contributed to these leadership challenges. Prioritizing intelligence may seem logical, but it often leads to the "Intelligence Trap," where reliance solely on cognitive abilities undermines leadership effectiveness and organizational success.

In today's competitive business landscape, organizations consistently prioritize intelligence quotient (IQ) in their hiring and promotion decisions. While this approach seems logical, it often leads to unintended consequences that undermine leadership effectiveness and organizational success.

The Traditional Path: From Expert to Leader

Organizations typically follow a predictable pattern in developing their leadership pipeline. They identify high-performing individuals – those who demonstrate superior technical or functional skills, problem-solving abilities, and domain expertise. These individuals receive extensive training and development opportunities to enhance their technical capabilities further. Many pursue advanced degrees or certifications to deepen their expertise.

This investment in technical or functional excellence creates a solid foundation of skilled professionals. However, a critical shift occurs when these experts are promoted into leadership positions. The very qualities that made them exceptional individual contributors – their deep functional knowledge and problem-solving abilities – may not translate directly into effective leadership skills.

The Promotion Paradox

Consider this common scenario: An engineer consistently delivers outstanding technical solutions, demonstrates innovative thinking, and maintains high-performance standards. Based on these achievements, they're promoted to lead a team of engineers. Suddenly, their role shifts from solving technical problems to leading people who solve technical problems – a fundamentally different challenge requiring a distinct skill set.

Such a transition often reveals a significant gap. While organizations invest heavily in technical training, they frequently provide minimal leadership development. New leaders find themselves in unfamiliar territory, armed with technical or functional expertise but lacking the tools to effectively guide, develop, and inspire their teams.

The Micromanagement Trap

The "micromanagement trap" permeates the dynamics faced by many new leaders. Often, these individuals come into leadership roles brimming with confidence in their functional skills. Their technical abilities haven't just brought them recognition; they've been the cornerstone of their career success thus far.

However, when it comes to leadership, these skills can become both a comfort and a constraint. Faced with the unknowns of managing people, they instinctively retreat to their area of expertise as a refuge, hoping to lead through the demonstration of their technical prowess, showing their team precisely how to execute tasks based on personal tried and true methodologies.

This can happen even at the highest levels. When he was an executive coach for startups, Rob Kornblum, co-author of this book and the president of CSI, used to ask new CEOs to imagine they had painted red paint on the bottom of their shoes. He would ask them, "At the end of the week, where would most of your steps be?" He found that people tend to gravitate to the function they know best. If they had been a great sales leader, they spent the most time in Sales. If they had been a great product leader or engineer, they tended to spend the most time around the Product Managers or Engineers.

This reliance on familiar processes, however, gives rise to several problematic behaviors that can hinder both the leader and his or her team's potential. New leaders often find themselves excessively involved in functional problems and decisions. Rather than empowering a team to navigate and interpret challenges, they dominate decision-making processes, thereby limiting creative problem solving. This micromanagement not only stifles the innovative spirit of the team, and it also overloads the leader, who then becomes a bottleneck in the workflow.

Furthermore, such leaders often struggle significantly with delegation. To them, releasing control feels synonymous with risking failure. This reluctance to delegate stems from a fear that others might not meet their standards or accomplish tasks in the precise manner they envision. As a result, they burden themselves with responsibilities that could nurture others' growth, and they end up experiencing burnout while at the same time they hamper the development of their team members' capacities.

Alongside this, there's typically a marked resistance to alternative approaches. Frequently, leaders entrenched in the micromanagement trap either consciously or subconsciously dismiss new ideas that deviate from their methods. This rigidity not only stifles creativity, it also prevents the organization from adapting quickly to change—which can be essential in a rapidly-evolving business environment.

Moreover, these leaders tend to focus more on task completion than on developing the people around them. Their ultimate goal becomes checking items off the to-do list rather than fostering a robust, capable team. With their focus on immediate task execution, long-term growth and development of team members is often neglected, causing the team to become less resilient and adaptable over time.

Finally, such individuals typically place significant emphasis on control rather than on team empowerment. The desire to maintain order can overshadow the need to inspire confidence and autonomy among team members. As a result, team members may feel disempowered or undervalued, which can dampen their motivation and stifle the innovation these leaders initially sought to promote.

Breaking free from this trap requires a conscious effort to shift focus from purely functional interventions to a more balanced approach that values empowerment, creativity, and personal development. Recognizing and mitigating these behaviors can result in to more effective, resilient leadership that fosters both individual and collective success.

The Hiring Challenge

The "Hiring Challenge" underscores a pervasive issue within organizational recruitment processes: the overreliance on Intelligence Quotient (IQ) factors when selecting candidates. This emphasis doesn't stop at promotion decisions—it is deeply embedded in the hiring practices themselves. Many organizations design their recruitment processes to heavily prioritize criteria such as educational qualifications, technical certifications, years of experience and domain expertise. These benchmarks undeniably serve to identify individuals who are technically proficient and can contribute effectively at an individual level.

However, such standardized criteria often fail to capture the essence of what makes an effective leader. The focus on academic achievements and past functional success tends to overshadow other non-tangible, yet crucial, leadership qualities such as emotional intelligence, adaptability, vision, problem solving, and the ability to inspire and motivate a team. The prevailing assumption that strong academic skills and individual success can seamlessly translate into exceptional leadership is a significant misconception. It places undue emphasis on IQrelated attributes while neglecting the nuanced, complex qualities that leaders need.

We see this issue come to the fore as early on as hiring for entry-level positions. Many companies require a college degree for entry-level jobs even when they don't truly require it based on the tasks involved. Those companies use "got into college, graduated from college" as a proxy for IQ.

Such an approach results in a critical challenge: developing leaders equipped for modern, dynamic organizational environments. The assumption that someone adept at functional tasks and armed with numerous qualifications will naturally evolve into a successful leader has led to the advancement and promotion of individuals who, while technically skilled, may lack the skills essential for effective leadership. This gap in leadership capability can be seen in poor team management, a lack of strategic vision, and an inability to foster a motivated and engaged workforce.

To address this challenge, organizations must broaden their recruitment lens. By valuing a diverse set of qualities such as emotional intelligence, collaborative spirit, strategic thinking, and resilience alongside technical skills, organizations can better identify individuals who not only excel as individual contributors but who also have the potential to become visionary leaders. This more holistic approach helps to cultivate a leadership pipeline rich in diversity and richness of thought, ensuring that the leaders of tomorrow are equipped to guide their teams through the complexities of an ever-changing business landscape.

The Leadership Pipeline Crisis

The "Leadership Pipeline Crisis" represents a significant challenge for many organizations today, characterized by a dwindling pool of willing leadership candidates. This shortage arises amid a growing hesitancy among high-performing technical professionals to step into leadership roles. These professionals often see a reality that is far from appealing—one marked by excessive workload and stress. Leadership, while offering the promise of increased influence and career advancement, increasingly appears to be accompanied by relentless pressure and unrelenting demands.

One of the most striking deterrents is the constant firefighting that occupies many leaders' time. Instead of strategic planning and visionary leadership, their waking hours are often consumed by the crisis of the day and other urgent operational issues. This kind of atmosphere not only stifles their ability to focus on long-term goals, it also creates a chaotic work environment with little room for thoughtful decision-making and innovation.

Moreover, potential leaders are acutely aware of the challenges their predecessors face in maintaining a healthy work-life balance. The blurred lines between personal and professional time, exacerbated by digital connectivity, leave little room for leaders to recharge, which increases the risk of burnout. This lack of balance poses a significant obstacle for those considering a transition from technical roles, where work may be more contained, to leadership roles with their all-consuming demands.

Additionally, there is a notable deficiency in support and development resources for leaders. Many organizations have yet to put in place comprehensive training and mentoring programs that could better prepare emerging leaders for their new roles. Without access to the necessary development tools and support structures, the path to leadership can seem daunting and unsupported.

There is an old joke that gets repeated so often it has become a meme:

CFO: "What if we invest all this money in our people through training and then they leave?"

CEO: "What if we don't, and then they stay?"

Alas, many companies allow the CFOs control of the budget to rule the day.

Finally, the expectations placed upon leaders are often disproportionately high compared to the preparation and resources provided. Leaders are expected to drive performance, foster innovation, and manage team dynamics effectively, and yet the investment in their readiness for these challenges is typically insufficient. This disconnect between expectation and preparation leaves many high-performing individuals skeptical about taking on leadership positions because they fear they would walk into roles with unrealistic demands and inadequate support.

To resolve this leadership pipeline crisis, organizations must re-evaluate and enrich their leadership development strategies. This involves not only redefining leadership roles to make them more sustainable, it also requires providing robust support systems, manageable workload expectations, and comprehensive leadership training. By cultivating an environment where leadership is seen not as an overwhelming burden but as a fulfilling and well-supported career path, organizations can encourage talented individuals to step into leadership roles confidently, thus ensuring a steady flow of capable leaders for the future.

Breaking the IQ-Only Paradigm

Organizations must evolve their approach to leadership development and selection to address these challenges. This requires:

1. Redefining Leadership Success:

First and foremost, organizations need to acknowledge that technical prowess alone does not equate to effective leadership. This requires redefining what leadership success looks like, recognizing the value of both technical experts and those with a talent for people leadership. To this end, organizations should develop distinct career paths that cater to both types of professionals.

By creating clear distinctions between functional and leadership roles, organizations can ensure that individuals are groomed and placed on tracks that best align with their strengths and aspirations. Such a nuanced approach can prevent the common pitfall where technical experts are pushed into leadership roles that are poor fits for them and thereby foster more satisfied and effective leaders.

2. Implementing Comprehensive Development Programs:

Because successful leadership begins with thorough preparation, organizations need to implement development programs that precede promotions. By introducing leadership training early in a professional's career, potential leaders can develop essential skills before stepping into leadership roles. Structured mentoring and coaching programs should be made available to provide critical support and guidance. A strong focus ought to be placed on cultivating people skills in addition to technical capabilities as well as programs offering real-world scenarios and feedback mechanisms. Moreover, organizations should create safe spaces where emerging leaders can practice their leadership skills without fear of significant repercussions, encouraging learning and growth through experience.

3. Revising Selection Criteria

The criteria for promoting individuals into leadership roles must evolve to include comprehensive indicators of leadership potential. Beyond technical skills, organizations should assess candidates' emotional intelligence (EQ) and Process Intelligence (PQ), both of which are vital for effective leadership in today's complex business environment. Including measures of a candidate's motivation and genuine desire to lead can also provide insight into their potential success in a leadership role. Furthermore, evaluating past experiences in team leadership or development can highlight a candidate's ability to lead effectively, offering a more holistic view of their capabilities.

It is not difficult to ask EQ or PQ questions of leader-ship candidates when querying their prior individual or leadership successes. This requires intentionality and peeling back the layers to determine why they were successful. Just doing this would open up broader pipelines of candidates for leadership positions.

4. Building Support Systems

To ensure the ongoing success of new leaders, organizations must establish robust support systems. In this regard, peer support networks can offer vital encourage-ment and shared learning experiences by creating a cohort of leaders who can navigate challenges together. Ongoing leadership coaching should be available, providing consistent expert guidance and a sounding board for new leaders. Establishing formal mentoring relationships can enhance this support, thereby pairing new leaders with experienced mentors who offer advice and impart valuable lessons. Additionally, organizations should offer regular opportunities for feedback and development, allowing leaders to continually refine their skills and adapt to new challenges.

By implementing these strategic changes, organizations can move beyond the limitations of an IQ-focused paradigm and nurture a generation of leaders equipped with the diverse skills necessary to thrive and innovate in today's dynamic business landscape.

The Path Forward

In the quest for effective leadership, it's imperative for organizations to reassess and broaden their selection and development criteria. While Intelligence Quotient (IQ) continues to hold value—providing the foundation necessary for strategic thinking and problem-solving—it cannot stand alone as the primary measure of a potential leader's capability. Today's complex business environment demands a more balanced and integrated approach, where leadership prowess hinges not only on IQ but also on Emotional Intelligence (EQ) and Process Intelligence (PQ).

Technical, Functional Competence (IQ):

IQ remains vital in leadership; it forms the core of analytical abilities, strategic insight, and complex problem-solving skills that leaders need to navigate technical challenges. Ensuring that leaders have a strong intellectual grounding helps organizations tackle intricate issues and drive informed decision-making.

Emotional Intelligence (EQ):

EQ introduces an essential layer of social awareness and relational skills, which are crucial for fostering communication, empathy, and team cohesion. Leaders with high EQ can nurture and help create encouraging environments that promote collaborative efforts and enhance employee engagement. They are adept at managing interpersonal relationships judiciously and empathetically, which is particularly important when it comes to building and nurturing motivated and dedicated teams.

Process Intelligence (PQ):

PQ is the lynchpin that binds IQ and EQ. Leaders with strong PQ possess the ability to design, implement, and refine systems and processes that create consistency and enable scalability. This form of intelligence focuses on operational excellence, ensuring that efforts are coordinated effectively across teams and are truly aligned with organizational objectives. It empowers leaders to manage growth sustainably and maintain high performance standards amid changing circumstances.

Integrating these Elements:

To successfully integrate these three core elements, organizations need their leadership development frameworks to recalibrate. This will likely require redesigning recruitment and training processes in order to balance out and enhance the levels of IQ, EQ, and PQ in prospective and current leaders. Doing so will not only prepare individuals for leadership responsibilities in the short term, it will ensure that a steady pipeline of candidates is created and maintained for the future.

Organizations also must embark on this journey with a commitment to evolving their leadership culture. Encouraging a blend of technical competence, emotional maturity, and process optimization within leadership roles will foster a resilient and adaptable environment. Such a comprehensive approach will equip leaders not only to face today's challenges but also to anticipate and prepare for demands that may arise in the future.

By acknowledging this reality and adjusting their approach accordingly, current leaders of organizations can better prepare their future leaders for success and create more sustainable leadership pipelines.

Conclusion

The practice of hiring and promoting primarily based on IQ has been common for many decades, but in today's complex business environment, it can no longer be depended upon to produce the most effective leaders. As a result, organizations must develop more nuanced approaches that take into account the full spectrum of leadership capabilities. This shift will not only produce more effective leaders but also create more appealing leadership paths for high-performing individuals.

The question isn't whether IQ matters; it certainly does. The question is whether it should remain the primary factor in identifying and developing future leaders. As we'll explore in subsequent chapters, creating truly effective leaders requires a more balanced and comprehensive approach.

By expanding the criteria for leadership selection to include Emotional Intelligence (EQ) and Process Intelligence (PQ), organizations can build dynamic teams led by individuals who inspire, engage, and innovate. Such evolution in leadership development will pave the way for a more resilient and adaptable organizational culture. Leaders attuned to their team's emotional needs, who can optimize processes effectively, are in position to navigate the rapid changes as well as the incredible complexities of the world of the business today.

Additionally, when organizations redefine their leadership frameworks in this way, they signal a commitment to inclusivity and diversity by acknowledging that diverse skills and perspectives are valuable assets. This fosters a sense of shared purpose and achievement, and it helps create a culture of continuous learning and adaptation, while at the same time empowering leaders to grow alongside their teams.

In summary, the path forward involves recognizing that truly effective leadership demands a holistic integration of intelligence types. By embracing this comprehensive approach, organizations can ensure robust leadership pipelines and sustain success in an ever-evolving global landscape.

WORKBOOK
Assessing and Developing Beyond IQ

Self-Assessment: Leadership Transition Readiness
Rate yourself on a scale of 1 (Strongly Disagree) to 5 (Strongly Agree):

Technical Excellence vs. Leadership Balance
I can effectively delegate tasks without needing to control the process ___
I spend more time developing people than solving technical problems ___
I'm comfortable with different approaches to achieving results ___
I can separate technical decisions from leadership responsibilities ___

Score: ___ / 20

Leadership Motivation
I have a genuine desire to develop others ___
I find satisfaction in team achievements more than personal technical accomplishments ___
I'm willing to step back from hands-on technical work

___

I'm excited about creating systems and processes for team success ___

Score: ___ / 20

Reflection Questions

What aspects of your current role do you find most energizing? Most draining?

How do you currently balance technical expertise with people development?

What leadership skills do you need to develop beyond your technical capabilities?

What support systems would help you become a more effective leader?

Action Planning

Technical Expertise Transition

List three ways you currently use your technical expertise:

Identify how each could be transformed into a development opportunity for your team:

Leadership Development Goals

Short-term (3 months):

Medium-term (6 months):

Long-term (12 months):

Support System Design

Mentorship needs:

Training requirements:

Resource gaps:

Network development:

Micromanagement Self-Check

Review your last week of work. Note instances where you:

Took over a task instead of coaching

Made decisions that could have been delegated

Spent time on technical details instead of people development

Commitment to Change

Based on this assessment, identify:

One behavior you will stop:

One behavior you will start:

One behavior you will continue:

Remember: Leadership development is a journey, not a destination. Regular reflection and adjustment are key to growth.

Chapter Three

We Train for EQ: The Emotional Intelligence Evolution & Breaking Free from Managing by Personality

Our journey into Process Intelligence Leadership began with the introduction of a groundbreaking framework comprising three dimensions: Intelligence Quotient (IQ), Emotional Intelligence (EQ), and Process Intelligence (PQ). We explored how traditional reliance on only IQ and EQ, while beneficial, leaves organizations at risk of becoming overly dependent on individual personalities. In Chapter Two, we investigated how organizations have historically favored an IQ-centric approach in leadership selection, often promoting functionally skilled individuals due to their intellectual strengths, which can lead to unintended pitfalls. Chapter Three will examine the shift from IQ-centric leadership to the embracing of EQ as an additional measure. Without underlying systems, however, EQ training can inadvertently affirm the very personality-dependence it seeks to mitigate. Recognizing this challenge is essential in order to understand the need to develop and nurture leaders capable of building sustainable and scalable organizations that operate effectively without relying on constant personal oversight.

PQ is the crucial element that bridges the gaps left by IQ and EQ-centric models. PQ enables leaders to design systems that naturally improve decision-making as well as collaborative work environments. By decentralizing tasks and promoting shared leadership, PQ alleviates reliance on individual capabilities, drastically minimizing burnout and inefficiency.

As we delve into PQ in this chapter, we will discover how it systematically leverages the strengths of both IQ and EQ to create a comprehensive leadership framework. This integrated approach prepares organizations to function resiliently and adaptively, independent of any single leader's continual presence. By embracing and instituting PQ, teams grow more unified, innovation thrives within structured systems, and organizations become poised to scale effectively while maintaining operational harmony.

What Is Emotional Intelligence?

Emotional intelligence refers to the ability to understand and manage your own emotions while also recognizing and influencing the emotions of others. Originally introduced in 1990 by researchers John Mayer and Peter Salovey, the concept gained widespread recognition through psychologist Daniel Goleman.

More than a decade ago, Goleman emphasized the critical role of emotional intelligence in leadership by stating in the *Harvard Business Review*: "The most effective leaders share one essential quality: a high level of emotional intelligence. While IQ and technical skills are important, they are merely baseline requirements for executive roles."

Goleman's work on Emotional Intelligence has significantly shaped how we understand and cultivate emotional and social skills. His framework is structured around four quadrants—Self-Awareness, Self-Management, Social Awareness, and Relationship Management—each containing competencies that can be developed to improve personal and interpersonal effectiveness.

The following text focuses on how these quadrants and 12 competencies relate to emotional self-awareness, emotional balance, empathy, and inspirational leadership:

1. Self-Awareness

Understanding Emotional Intelligence requires an awareness of your own emotions and how they affect your thoughts and actions. In other words, figuratively speaking, it's important to step back and become self-aware. Emotional self-awareness involves recognizing your emotions, identifying their triggers, and understanding how they influence your behavior. To develop this skill, it's best to start by practicing mindfulness, which requires focusing on and staying aware of the present moment without allowing judgment to creep into your thoughts.

2. Self-Management

Self-management is a crucial component of Emotional Intelligence in that it requires focusing on controlling one's emotions and behaviors. At its core is Emotional Balance, also known as Emotional Self-Control. A short gap in time exists between an event that triggers an emotion and the onset of emotion itself. It's possible to use this gap to stop, think, and to reflect in order to quell the disruptive impulse—thereby remaining calm and composed under pressure.

3. Social Awareness

Social Awareness revolves around understanding the emotions and needs of others, as well as what is taking place in the surrounding environment. To develop empathy, it's important to practice active listening by not interrupting, and instead, concentrating intently on what someone is saying.

4. Relationship Management

Relationship Management focuses on leveraging emotional awareness to build and sustain strong, positive connections with others. To enhance skills in inspirational leadership, it's important to practice authentic communication, i.e., to be genuine and transparent in your interactions.

The Twelve Competencies of Emotional Intelligence

Daniel Goleman's emotional intelligence framework encompasses twelve vital competencies that form the foundation of effective leadership and personal development. It begins with **emotional self-awareness**, which is the cornerstone competency. Leaders must learn to step back, figuratively speaking,in order to recognize and understand their own emotional states. This allows them to accurately assess how their feelings influence their thoughts, behaviors, and decision-making processes.

Emotional balance, which builds upon the emotional self-awareness foundation, is the ability to maintain composure and clarity in stressful situations. This is particularly crucial during times of crisis or significant change.

Achievement orientation drives individuals to continuously improve and strive for excellence. This competency manifests as an internal motivation to set and pursue challenging goals, maintain high standards, and seek opportunities for growth. Leaders with strong achievement orientation inspire a similar drive in their teams, thereby creating a culture of continuous improvement and excellence.

Adaptability is next. It enables leaders to remain flexible and effective in the face of new challenges.

A Positive Outlook complements adaptability and is the ability to see opportunities in difficult circumstances. Leaders who maintain optimism while remaining realistic can inspire confidence and resilience in their teams.

Empathy: Empathetic leaders create strong bonds with their teams, they make more inclusive decisions, and they foster environments in which team members feel understood and valued.

Organizational Awareness enables leaders to navigate complex social and political dynamics within their institutions. It involves understanding power relationships, decision-making networks, and organizational culture.

Competency of Influence: Leaders skilled in influence are able to articulate compelling visions, build support for initiatives, and guide others toward shared goals without relying on the authority of their position alone.

The **Coach and Mentor** competency focuses on developing others' capabilities and potential.

Conflict Management enables leaders to address disagreements and tensions constructively by helping parties reach mutually beneficial resolutions.

Inspirational Leadership ties many other competencies together thereby enabling leaders to create positive change and to motivate others to embrace shared objectives. It involves articulating compelling visions, generating enthusiasm.

Finally, **Teamwork** promotes collaboration, mutual support, and collective achievement. Leaders skilled in teamwork create environments where cooperation flourishes and diverse perspectives are valued.

These twelve competencies work synergistically, each supporting and enhancing the others. In today's complex business environment, these emotional intelligence competencies distinguish exceptional leaders from average ones.

Managing by Personality
The Three P's in Action

Position: The Authority Trap

Leaders in today's complex economy face many challenges—acting as coaches, mentors, facilitators, mediators, educators, schedulers, HR persons, and motivators. They are asked to do more with less while motivating their teams to meet organizational goals. With so many demands, most leaders default to managing by personality, which manifests through the three key approaches previously discussed: Position, Proximity, and Persuasion.

When leaders rely on title and authority ("Do it because I said so!") they create organizations dependent on their personal presence. Consider this story:

Two friends were talking about their work situations. One lamented that nothing was going right.

"Why is that?" his friend asked. "I thought your department was the sweetheart of the company."

"It was," replied the first. "But a few weeks ago, the vice president in charge of our department left. And now everything is in chaos. No one is starting new projects because they're waiting for the new boss to tell them what to do. They don't want to start something and have it squashed later. Everything has ground to a halt."

This company's dependence on the leader's personality, expressed through position and authority, created organizational paralysis when that leader departed.

Proximity: The Presence Problem

The second manifestation of personality-dependent management is the belief that work only happens when the leader is physically present. A manager recently shared this revealing story:

"We were communicating with a manager whose company's headquarters are in England. For days, calls and emails went unanswered. Finally, we heard from him: 'Sorry I haven't been in touch. The top brass from London are expected next week. You can imagine how hectic it's been around here preparing for the visit."

The approach of "management by walking around" is generally a good one. We have certainly all been trained that it is. It can help leaders validate what they think to be true, and help build relationships and empathy. Where it falls down, however, is that organizations become dependent on the physical presence of specific personalities to build and maintain performance.

Persuasion: The Personal Influence Challenge

The third expression of personality-dependent management is relying on personal persuasion to get work done. As one supervisor confided:

"Look, I've learned the hard way, 'If you want something done, do it yourself.' By the time I convinced someone on my staff that it had to be done, I could have finished it myself. Arguing over it just isn't worth the effort."

This leader, like many others, was trapped in a cycle of personal intervention and persuasion.

Issues with The Three "Ps"

We have been schooled to think that leadership is about *the person.* From military leaders like Napoleon or Eisenhower, to government leaders like Thatcher or Kennedy, to business leaders like Jack Welch at GE or Indra Nooyi at PepsiCo, all had a commanding presence and a deep sense of their company's strategic direction. This is "The Three Ps" in action. Their personality and position was key, sometimes deferring proximity to their direct reports.

But, as we have pointed out, without *leadership systems* underlying their 3Ps, organizations can falter once those leaders move on. And they will. Top talent either gets promoted inside, or gets poached to other companies. Organizations cannot sustain success without PQ in place to keep a leader's business unit success alive once they move on.

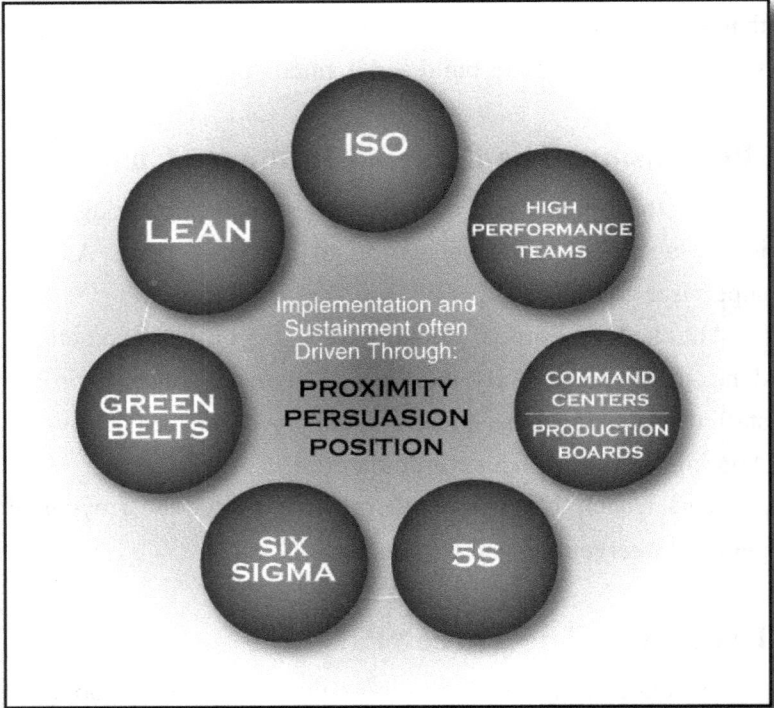

Implementation and Sustainment often Driven Through:

PROXIMITY
PERSUASION
POSITION

(ISO, LEAN, HIGH PERFORMANCE TEAMS, COMMAND CENTERS / PRODUCTION BOARDS, 5S, SIX SIGMA, GREEN BELTS)

The Firefighter Fallacy: A Cautionary Tale

During a recent client visit, I encountered a stark example of how organizations inadvertently reinforce personality-dependent management. The Training and Development Manager proudly described their leadership development program for new supervisors—a five-day intensive course that culminated with each graduate receiving a firefighter's helmet, ceremonially signed by the plant manager.

While well-intentioned, this ritual perfectly encapsulated everything wrong with traditional leadership development. The message was clear: successful supervisors were expected to be heroic firefighters, rushing from crisis to crisis, wielding their position's authority to give orders, using their physical presence to oversee operations, and applying personal persuasion to extinguish problems.

This approach not only celebrated, it actually institutionalized the Three P's of personality management. By equipping supervisors with "firefighting" skills, the organization was unknowingly creating a self-perpetuating cycle. Leaders trained to be crisis managers *will inevitably find themselves managing crises—rather than building systems and processes that prevent fires in the first place.*

The irony was striking: in attempting to develop strong leaders, they were instead reinforcing a dependency on individual personality-driven management styles. True organizational resilience doesn't come from having the best firefighters—it comes from building fire-resistant structures and installing effective sprinkler systems. In other words, sustainable leadership requires moving beyond the Three P's to create robust systems that function regardless of who holds the helmet.

This anecdote serves as a powerful reminder that many organizations still mistake crisis management for leadership, unknowingly perpetuating the very problems they're trying to solve. The path forward requires fundamentally rethinking how to develop leaders—not as emergency responders, but as architects of sustainable, personality-independent systems.

The EQ Training Paradox

As organizations grappled with the limitations of IQ-heavy leadership models, many saw EQ training as the remedy. While the intention was to cultivate more emotionally intelligent leaders, the approach often led to unexpected challenges, birthing what we now understand as the EQ training paradox.

In practice, traditional EQ training has a tendency to prioritize personal relationship building. While fostering strong interpersonal connections is valuable, relying too heavily on individual relationships can create a management style that's dependent on personal warmth and charisma. This focus can inadvertently overshadow the need for structured, systematic approaches that ensure consistency and sustainability across the organization.

Moreover, much of EQ training historically concentrated on developing emotional skills at an individual level. While important, this often came at the expense of establishing broader emotional systems at the organizational level. Without systems in place to support emotional intelligence on a larger scale, the impact of training often became fragmented, benefiting individual leaders without necessarily benefiting the entire organization.

Lastly, EQ training often prepares leaders to excel in personal intervention, guiding them to resolve issues through direct involvement. This approach, though helpful in specific situations, can be at the expense of and thereby negate the development of sustainable processes that allow teams to function smoothly and independently. Organizations can become overly reliant on individual leaders to maintain harmony and resolve conflicts as a result.

To fully capitalize on EQ's potential, organizations need to move beyond focusing solely on personal competencies. They need to develop comprehensive systems that embed emotional intelligence into the fabric of the organization, thereby ensuring that the benefits of EQ training are both widespread and sustainable.

Breaking Free: From Personality to Process

To ensure organizations thrive on an ongoing basis, leaders need to shift from personality-dependent management to systematic approaches that empower the entire organization.

First, the focus should be on replacing personal authority with process authority. Rather than relying on individual decision-makers, organizations can create clear decision frameworks that empower teams to act confidently and consistently. Establishing standard operating procedures ensures that everyone knows how to handle routine tasks, while systematic problem-solving approaches provide a structured method for tackling challenges as they arise.

Next, leaders should focus on transitioning from personal presence to systems presence. Implementing performance monitoring systems allows for the consistent and objective evaluation of progress, which ensures that success is driven by the collective rather than an individual's charisma. Structured accountability processes keep everyone aligned with organizational goals, while automated tracking mechanisms provide real-time data, helping teams to make informed decisions efficiently.

Finally, leaders have to examine the degree in which they are utilizing their "powers of persuasion." In essence, how much does engagement require the leader to cajole, convince, conspire utilizing their powers of persuasion to get individuals and teams to engage. Too often, leaders fall into the "Persuasion Trap" where we default to going to the same willing participants over and over, while intentionally working around those who are more difficult and less willing to engage. It doesn't take much convincing to get someone who is already engaged to do more. Most likely they are willing and eager. Every leader loves the colleague who is easy to engage. Consequently, every team has those individuals who are less likely to engage and no amount of cajoling or convincing is going to have a lasting effect. The effort to persuade these folks takes time, patience, and fortitude and in an ever demanding leadership environment, it is often easier to default to the willing than engage the unwilling. Another consequence is that many leaders being in possession of both IQ and EQ, know this model of engagement isn't productive or fair. It creates a culture of engagement disparity. Too often leaders understand the consequence or persuasion but lack the time or energy to confront this disparity so they default to "its just easier and faster if I do it myself." So at the end of the day when leaders desperately need to create cultures of collective accountability, they often default to selective engagement. The consequences of persuasion often fall squarely on the shoulders of the leaders as they are building cultures of dependency, not accountability.

The Manufacturing Merger: Breaking Free from Personality-Dependent Integration

When Regional Manufacturing Corp acquired Midwest Production Solutions, a competitor of equal size, the challenges were immediate and significant. Both companies had strong cultures and successful track records, but their approaches were markedly different. Regional was known for its aggressive, results-driven culture, while Midwest had built its reputation on careful, methodical processes.

The Initial Crisis

In many divisions, the integration process unfolded in a familiar pattern marked by personality-dependent management. Division heads found themselves personally mediating every conflict, believing that their hands-on approach would prevent issues from escalating. Meanwhile, managers dedicated countless hours to one-on-one meetings, attempting to smooth over tensions and to foster a sense of unity.

In an effort to bridge cultural gaps, leaders exhausted themselves through relentless personal interventions, striving personally to connect disparate teams. However, these well-intentioned efforts often fell short, as reliance on personal relationships did not always work out as intended and this resulted in inconsistency and uncertainty.

As this dynamic persisted, top performers from both companies began to leave, driven away by the instability and lack of clear direction. Within just six months, the results were alarming: productivity had plummeted by 30% in most divisions, and employee turnover had doubled. The organization's reliance on personality-driven management not only had failed to achieve integration, it had compounded the challenges.

Linda Chen's Different Approach

During the integration, Linda Chen, Operations Director for the Western Division, recognized the pitfalls of personality-dependent management. She opted for a radically different strategy and introduced Process Based Leadership® as the way to create and sustain a collaborative and cohesive culture.

Her approach involved creating frameworks and processes that facilitated clarity and connectivity across the division, without relying solely on personal interactions. In doing so, she aimed to foster a cohesive environment where everyone felt connected to the key metrics that bound them together in common cause. Linda's implementation of Process Based Leadership® was designed to ensure a consistent, scalable, and sustainable business process which in turn led to a positive and affirming organizational culture.

1. Cultural Integration System

Rather than rely on personal intervention, Linda decided to create a structured process. Recognizing the need for consistent communication, she organized weekly cross-company team meetings guided by a standardized agenda intended to foster collaboration and to address issues collectively. She also initiated "best practice sharing" sessions, which allowed representatives from each company to highlight and document their unique capabilities. This not only enabled everyone to leverage the strengths of both organizations, it led to greater understanding between the groups, and it promoted mutual respect.

2. Pulse Survey System

Linda introduced an automated pulse survey system with weekly anonymous pulse surveys to gather specific feedback on integration challenges. The surveys provided real-time insights into potential issues or problems, enabling the team to address concerns proactively.

An important feature of this system was the automated flagging of emerging issues, which allowed them to be identified and addressed before reaching a critical stage. In cases where any metric fell below a predetermined threshold, response protocols were put in place to ensure prompt corrective action.

Public reporting of survey results and subsequent actions took place on a regular basis in order to maintain transparency and trust. This fostered accountability, and it also demonstrated the company's commitment to ongoing improvement and employee well-being. This resulted in the integration process becoming more agile, responsive, and transparent.

3. Mentorship System

Linda also implemented CSI's Leadership GPS®, a long-term leadership development program which created a focus on emerging leaders and strong mentorship of existing leaders. This fostered purposeful connections across the company while developing the next level leaders within the organization. As a component of the Leadership GPS® program, she instituted formal mentor-mentee pairings that bridged company lines, thereby encouraging cross-organizational learning and collaboration.

To ensure the effectiveness of these pairings, clear expectations and meeting schedules were established, providing a framework for consistent and meaningful interactions. Documented discussion topics and progress tracking were integral to the system, which allowed mentees and mentors to focus on key development areas and monitor progress over time.

Additionally, regular rotation of mentorship pairings was implemented to help individuals build broader networks and gain diverse perspectives. This approach not only enriched individual development, it also strengthened the organizational culture by cultivating a cohesive and interconnected workforce. Through the Leadership GPS® program, personal and professional growth was strategically supported and enhanced.

4. Issue Resolution System

In addition, Linda set up a streamlined issue resolution system to ensure that concerns were addressed promptly and effectively. She introduced an online portal specifically for submitting integration issues. This provided employees with a straightforward and accessible way to report problems as they arose.

The system mandated an initial response time of 48 hours, guaranteeing that each issue would be acknowledged and addressed swiftly. The resolution process for each issue was meticulously tracked, with clear ownership assigned, ensuring accountability and transparency throughout the process.

To maintain open communication with employees, Linda also issued regular public updates on the progress of issue resolution. This approach not only demonstrated the company's commitment to addressing concerns, it also fostered trust and collaboration across the organization. Through this Issue Resolution System, the process of identifying and resolving challenges became transparent, efficient, and responsive.

The Results

After six months of implementing these changes, Linda's division stood out as a model of successful integration while other divisions continued to face challenges. Remarkably, productivity in her division increased by 15% compared to pre-merger levels, which was definitely a testament to the effectiveness of her approach.

In reflection of the positive work environment and stability she cultivated, the employee turnover rate of her division dropped to just 5% in contrast to the 25% seen company-wide. Moreover, employee satisfaction scores soared beyond what they had been before the merger, indicating a more engaged and content workforce.

Linda also achieved a successful integration of best practices from both companies, thereby harnessing their combined strengths and enhancing overall performance. Through her innovative systems, Linda not only navigated the complexities of merger integration but also fostered a thriving and cohesive division.

Key Learning: The Power of Systems Over Personality

When asked about her success, Linda explained:

"Everyone else was trying to manage this merger through personal relationships and individual intervention. But you can't scale that approach across hundreds of employees. We needed systems that would work whether I was personally involved or not."

She also added a crucial insight:

"The irony is that by creating systems, we actually improved relationships more than if we'd focused on relationships directly. People felt secure because they knew exactly how things worked, how to raise concerns, and how they would be addressed. That security created the space for genuine relationships to develop naturally."

Long-term Impact

Two years after the merger, Regional Manufacturing Corp adopted Linda's approach company-wide. The key lesson? Cultural integration doesn't depend on charismatic leaders or personal intervention. It requires robust systems that can operate independently of any individual's presence or personality.

As Linda often says, "Good systems create good cultures. Good personalities are a bonus, but good systems are essential."

Similar praise was echoed by Hans Peter, President & CEO of Phenix Label, who said, "In my 38 years of leading Phenix Label, nothing has been more impactful than the sustainable systems and processes we developed with Shane and CSI. The consistency of his methodology allowed us to replicate excellence, address problems so they were never repeated, and build a foundation where accountability and engagement became the norm. Today, we continue to use those tools to prosper and sustain our competitive advantage, and I am now passing them on to my son Charlie as he prepares to lead Phenix into its fifth generation as a family-owned business. Shane and CSI didn't just help us hit goals in the short term, they gave us the processes to transform how we lead and ensure that our success carries on well into the future."

Conclusion

Emotional intelligence remains a crucial leadership component, but its true power emerges when integrated with robust processes and systems. In order to thrive, organizations must move beyond simply training for EQ to creating environments where emotional intelligence can thrive at scale.

The question isn't whether EQ matters—it does. The question is how to make emotional intelligence sustainable and scalable through proper systems and processes. As we'll explore in upcoming chapters, integrating EQ with PQ creates leaders who can maintain an emotional connection while building sustainable, scalable organizations.

Workbook
Breaking Free from
Managing by Personality

Part 1: The Three P's Self-Assessment

Rate yourself on a scale of 1 (Rarely) to 5 (Frequently):

Position-Based Management

I rely on my title or authority to get things done ___

My team waits for my approval before acting ___

Decision-making stops when I'm unavailable ___

People defer to my position rather than following processes ___

Score: ___ / 20

Proximity-Based Management

Work quality improves when I'm physically present ___

Team performance drops when I'm away ___

I need to "walk around" to ensure tasks are completed ___

Problems wait for my return to be resolved ___

Score: ___ / 20

Persuasion-Based Management

I personally convince team members to take on tasks ___

I rely on specific "go-to" people to get things done ___

I spend significant time explaining why work needs to be done ___

I end up doing tasks myself to avoid convincing others ___

Score: ___ / 20

Part 2: System Readiness Assessment

Rate your organization's current state: 1 (No System) to 5 (Robust System)

Decision-Making Systems

Clear decision frameworks exist ___

Standard operating procedures are documented ___

Problem-solving processes are standardized ___

Escalation paths are well-defined ___

Performance Management Systems

Automated performance tracking exists ___

Accountability processes are documented ___

Quality control systems are in place ___

Feedback mechanisms are systematic ___

Engagement Systems

Motivation systems are standardized ___

Consequence management is systematic ___

Communication protocols are established ___

Team building is process-driven ___

Part 3: Breaking Free Action Planning

Current State Analysis

List three ways you currently manage by personality:

Identify the costs of these approaches:

Time costs:

Emotional costs:

Organizational costs:

Future State Design

For each P (Position, Proximity, Persuasion), identify one
system to develop:

Position: From _____ to _____

System needed:

Resources required:

Timeline:

Proximity: From _____ to _____

System needed:

Resources required:

Timeline:

Persuasion: From _____ to _____

System needed:

Resources required:

Timeline:

Part 4: Implementation Planning

30-Day Actions

What one system will you start building immediately?

What resources do you need?

How will you measure success?

90-Day Goals

Which personality-dependent practices will you eliminate?

What systems will replace them?

How will you track progress?

One-Year Vision

How will your leadership look different?

What systems will be fully operational?

How will your team function differently?

Part 5: Resistance and Challenges

What obstacles do you anticipate?

From yourself:

From your team:

From the organization:

How will you address each obstacle?

Personal strategies:

Team strategies:

Organizational strategies:

Part 6: Support Requirements

What training do you need?

Who needs to be involved?

What resources are required?

Commitment to Change

I commit to replacing the following personality-dependent practices with systems:

Instead of _____, I will create _____.

Instead of _____, I will implement _____.

Instead of _____, I will develop _____.

Review Date: _____

Remember: The goal is not to eliminate personality and emotional intelligence but to create systems that make them sustainable and scalable.

Monthly Progress Check

Track your progress monthly:

Month 1:

    Systems implemented:

    Challenges encountered:

    Adjustments needed:

Month 2:

    Systems implemented:

    Challenges encountered:

    Adjustments needed:

Month 3:

    Systems implemented:

    Challenges encountered:

    Adjustments needed

Chapter Four
The Secret Superpower,
Process Intelligence

As we've seen, organizations have moved from valuing just IQ to recognizing EQ as a pivotal part of leadership. This shift fundamentally changed how we understand effective leadership—it's not enough to be functionally brilliant. Those skills alone can't address complex issues like team dynamics, employee engagement, or sustainable performance.

Adopting EQ into management practices has helped develop leaders who can relate better to their teams, understand diverse emotions, and nurture healthier workplace environments. But even with these benefits, EQ training has its limitations. It can often swap out one dependency for another—emphasizing leaders' emotional skills over other competencies—making departments vulnerable when these emotionally savvy leaders left or burned out.

Here is the central challenge: maintain and sustain technical and emotional excellence without relying on specific people. The solution isn't more training in IQ or EQ alone but integrating both within the organization. Process Intelligence involves the creation of durable systems. It takes the knowledge from IQ and the interpersonal skills from EQ and weaves them into a scalable framework that strengthens the entire organization.

With PQ, organizations move beyond individual brilliance. They build systems that incorporate knowledge and emotional insight into every layer of the organization. PQ ensures that processes are not only well-designed but are adaptable enough to meet future challenges.

By institutionalizing these strengths, PQ allows organizations to thrive regardless of changes in leadership, creating resilience that's embedded in the organization's DNA and ensuring sustainable success that can outlast any single leader's tenure.

The Leadership Triangle: Completing the Picture

PQ isn't just another leadership skill to add to the toolkit. It is a fundamental capability that allows organizations to fully leverage both IQ and EQ, to create systems and processes that enable consistent, scalable, and sustainable success

For decades, leaders of organizations have operated on the assumption that combining technical expertise with emotional intelligence would create the perfect leader. As we've seen, however, this two-dimensional approach leaves organizations vulnerable to personality-dependent management, which can result in unsustainable success. Process Intelligence emerges as the third critical dimension, completing what can be called the Leadership Triangle.

The Distinct Nature of Process Intelligence

Process Intelligence (PQ) stands apart from its counterparts, IQ and EQ, by fundamentally reorienting the focus from the skills and aptitudes of individuals to organizational processes and systems.

Where IQ emphasizes the breadth and depth of what we know—our ability to analyze, evaluate, and create based on technical understanding—and EQ hones in on how we navigate interpersonal dynamics and influence and empathize with others,

PQ shifts toward the broader application and integration of these skills within an organization.

How PQ Complements IQ and EQ

We know that IQ is crucial for identifying what needs to be accomplished within an organization. As we have seen, however, without a supporting framework, brilliant leaders can inadvertently become bottlenecks, as their unique skills and insights are not effectively disseminated. PQ addresses this by creating systems and processes that capture and standardize their functional knowledge. This ensures that their expertise is not only understood, but that it can be applied consistently and scaled throughout the organization. It allows for knowledge to become shared and replicable, rather than concentrated and singular.

Emotional intelligence is vital for building and managing relationships. Yet, there is a risk that business success becomes solely reliant on individual emotional skills. PQ alleviates this by turning EQ from a personal asset into a lasting organizational capability. It does this by embedding emotional intelligence into the frameworks and the processes of the organization, ensuring that the ability to understand and manage complex emotional dynamics is ingrained in the corporate culture. This transition reduces dependency on individual leaders' emotional intuitions and ensures that supportive, emotionally intelligent interactions are consistently part of everyday operations.

In other words, through PQ, both IQ and EQ can be promoted with the result that organizational health will be sustainable and leadership more effective.

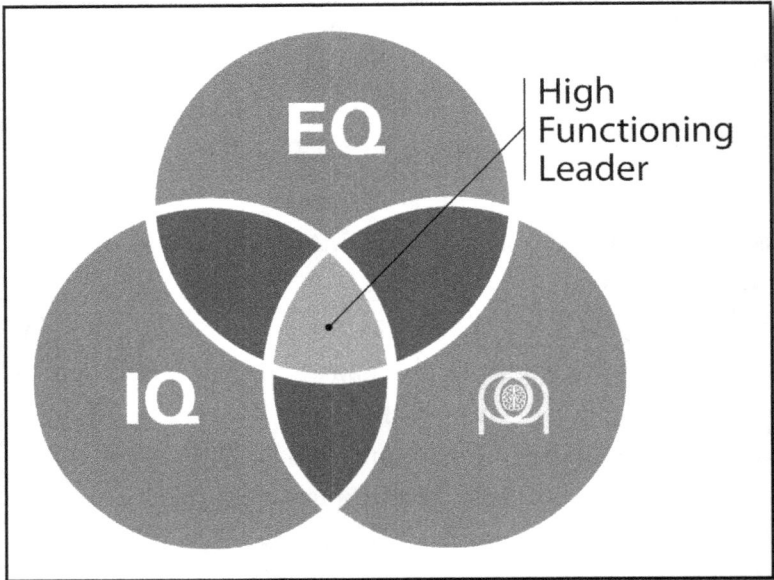

Key Distinctions of PQ:

Systems Thinking vs. Individual Action

Imagine you're faced with a challenge at work. With an IQ approach, you'd rely on your expertise, thinking, "I know how to solve this problem." Your deep understanding enables you to dissect the issue, apply logic, and arrive at a solution based on your knowledge.

Now, consider the EQ perspective, where the focus is on interpersonal dynamics. Here, you'd think, "I can help people work together to solve this problem." Your emotional intelligence enables you to navigate group interactions, fostering collaboration and helping team members contribute effectively by understanding each other's strengths and emotions.

Shift to the PQ perspective and your viewpoint transforms. Instead of relying on individual expertise or the power of collaboration alone, you think, "I can create a system that enables people to solve this problem, and similar problems, consistently." Here, the emphasis is on systems thinking.

You work on developing structures and processes that harness both IQ and EQ, ensuring that the problem-solving capabilities are ingrained in the organization. This approach seeks to capture and institutionalize effective strategies, making sure that anyone in the organization can tackle similar challenges with the same success, without having to rely on any one individual's skills or presence.

Scalability vs. Personal Presence

Leaders typically want their businesses to grow. With global markets, and the ability to reach customers and consumers instantly through the Internet, the opportunities for growth have never been greater. Consider the speed of adoption of mobile phones, social media, and AI tools. All have reached billions of users in record time.

Growing businesses need leaders who can scale, not only their own organizations, but also the ability to be promoted inside the company in order to take on new and greater responsibilities.

When organizations rely too heavily on IQ, knowledge often ends up trapped within the minds of experts who possess specialized skills. While these individuals are invaluable, their expertise remains largely inaccessible to others, limiting the organization's ability to leverage this knowledge on a broader scale. On the other hand, an EQ-focused approach emphasizes building strong relationships and fostering collaboration, but it has its own constraints. The effectiveness of these relationships is often dependent on the leadership style and personal presence of those skilled in emotional intelligence. When these leaders leave, or get promoted, the relationships they nurtured will likely falter, creating a void in team communication and problem solving. Business performance will likely also falter as a result.

This is where the advantage of Process Intelligence becomes evident. PQ involves the creation of systems that transcend individual expertise and personal relationships, ensuring that organizational processes and capabilities are not hindered by the absence of key individuals. By embedding knowledge and relationship-building skills within systemic frameworks, PQ enables the organization to continue to function effectively, regardless of who is present. This approach allows for scalable growth and adaptability, as the systems in place empower teams to maintain consistent performance and success, independent of any particular leader's presence.

Sustainability vs. Situational Success

The pursuit of success often varies in focus depending on the approach adopted. With an IQ-centered approach, the emphasis is on finding the right answer. Individuals leverage their expertise and analytical skills to solve problems, often achieving situational success by addressing immediate issues accurately and efficiently. However, the focus remains on problem-solving in the here and now.

In contrast, an EQ-oriented approach concentrates on managing the current situation by effectively navigating team dynamics and fostering positive relationships. Leaders skilled in EQ work to understand and respond to the emotional and interpersonal elements at play, ensuring harmonious outcomes in the moment. While highly effective during the immediate situation, this approach often relies heavily on the leader's presence and influence to maintain balance and cohesion.

"What got us here isn't going to get us there!"

Have you heard that statement before, or perhaps experienced that feeling? All the long hours, hard work, fortitude, wins and losses, and now, just when you think you achieved the summit, you look in the distance and realized you haven't reached the summit at all. The pace of change and the tempo of progress isn't slowing down, it's accelerating daily and too often, "What got us here, won't get us there!" This is often the challenge with scaling a business.

Having the strong entrepreneurial spirit is what made America the dominant industrial powerhouse that it is today. The attributes of grit, determination, and fortitude are admirable and required to succeed. So why do so many businesses fail to scale after a period of time? Our data suggests that while an entrepreneurial spirit is awesome, it often leaves unsustainable outcomes. That person or people who gave it their all, did it all, slept very little, sacrificed constantly, and never said "no" are simply burned out. The entrepreneurial badge of honor can at times feel like a weighted chain. Too often the culprit of these feelings is the lack of a good system to demonstrate to the leader that their physical proximity, powers of persuasion, and position authority are ultimately temporary and fleeting.

You might get to the first summit, but often leaders are too exhausted to make it to the second summit. Only through solid and simple systems can entrepreneurs ultimately get to the second summit. "What got us here, WILL NOT get us there" – The sooner we realize that truth the quicker we can build the systems necessary to scale, sustain, and succeed.

PQ takes this a step further by prioritizing the creation of repeatable processes that assure consistent success over time. With PQ, the focus is not just on solving a specific problem or smoothing over a current situation, but on developing systems that embed these solutions into the fabric of the organization. This strategic foresight and emphasis on sustainability ensures that success isn't situational or fleeting but is enduring and adaptable to future challenges. By creating processes that can be replicated and adapted, PQ guarantees that organizations can thrive beyond individual successes or situational management, thereby leading to sustained growth and resilience.

We believe that technology is a key enabler to create processes that are scalable. We are not believers in "technology for its own sake"- it is easy to drown in data, or to let the tools drive you rather than you driving them. At a minimum, a set of dashboards is needed in order to tell those in the organization where they stand—whether they "are winning or losing." In addition, a tool is needed to record actions that *come from* your review of the metrics.

Demonstrating Sustainable Success

**CASE STUDY – The Army's Organic Industrial Base –
Creating a Battle Rhythm of Sustainable Business Processes**

Since 1994, CSI has been working within the United States Army, specifically within Army Materiel Command and its 23 Depots, Arsenals, and Ammunition Plants. In 1994, Tobyhanna Army Depot hired CSI to support them during a Congressionally launched Base Realignment and Closure Commission (BRAC).

CSI's charge was to teach this organization of 5,000 civilians and military personnel how to operate like private industry. Specifically with the design, documentation, and deployment of Non-Negotiable Business Processes utilizing CSI's Process Based Leadership® methodology. This initial engagement has led to decades of continued progress, performance, and readiness of Tobyhanna Army Depot. Through war time surges to peace time tempos, Tobyhanna Army Depot became the model of a high functioning organization within Army Materiel Command. In 2021, Army Materiel Command asked CSI to create a program to teach the other 22 installations the fundamentals of Process Intelligence and Process Based Leadership®. In these installations, civilians produce bombs and missiles while repairing and overhauling everything from weapons to tanks and everything in between. The capability of the Organic Industrial Base is mindblowing in its complexity while serving as our nation's "Arsenal of Democracy."

These Army installations are led by senior Army officers typically a Colonel who commands thousands of civilian employees. The Installation Commander rotates out every two years. The ability of each of these installations to have a PQ process driven by Process Based Leadership® to allow every two years the new Commander to "Step into a Way of Work" has been a key driver or organization success and operational readiness. In the past, every time a senior leader changed, the organizational systems had to be rebuilt to address the new personality.

Today, leaders at all levels are onboarded to the PQ process so they are indoctrinated into a way of work on Day One. This creates consistency, clarity, and connectivity across the installations. As a result, the system facilitates sustainable processes that don't depend solely on the organizations leader. A recent Commander recently noted, "For the first time in my Army career, I feel I can put down my rucksack and step into a system that is driving shared high functioning behaviors and processes. So often, my first year is spent trying to build a process to give me what I need only to see that process atrophy within weeks upon my departure. I now get to operate in a "growth mindset" where I can use my IQ and EQ to improve an existing system, not build one from scratch."

Core Components of Process Intelligence

Process Intelligence comprises several essential components that together enable leaders to create sustainable, scalable organizations:

1. System Design Intelligence

This is the ability to spot where an organization needs systems and then to design processes that work.

What it involves:

- Identifying where systems are needed by understanding current workflows and pinpointing areas that would benefit from structure
- Designing processes that are both reliable and flexible—reliable enough to work consistently, flexible enough to adapt to new challenges
- Creating frameworks that can grow and evolve with the organization
- Building in feedback loops so processes continuously improve

Making it simpler: Think of this as being the architect of how work gets done. You're not just solving today's problems. You're building the blueprint for how similar problems will be solved tomorrow.

2. Implementation Intelligence

Implementation Intelligence is the ability to bring theoretical systems into being and make them practical. In other words, making the new systems actually work in the real world.

What it involves:

- Rolling out new systems effectively with clear planning and execution
- Getting people on board by communicating benefits and involving stakeholders in planning
- Managing change periods by addressing resistance, providing training, and supporting people through transitions
- Continuously monitoring and adjusting based on real-time feedback
- Creating a Go Live date

As the organization navigates the transition periods, the role of change management becomes paramount. Leaders must manage these periods with finesse, addressing resistance, facilitating comprehensive training, and ensuring everyone is comfortable with the new processes. Clear, ongoing communication is key to assist team members during the adaptation phase.

How to Get the Right Metrics

The right metrics can be transformational. The wrong metrics can be disastrous. Too often metrics are set based on two events – the beginning of the year or a problem. While logical on the surface, each of these two scenarios can often lead to metrics that operate more like a thermometer rather than a thermostat. To truly create Transformational Metrics, the right process isn't an exercise in Visualization, it's an exercise in Utilization. Metrics become Thermostatic when organizations build a Utilization Process that includes the following elements:

Educate – Embedding the metrics into the Learning and Development process. Teaching leaders why the metrics matter, where they come from and how they influence performance.

Facilitate – Thermostatic metrics should be the key facilitator of the meeting agenda – "Are we winning or losing?"

Iterate – The content of conversation must be equivalent to the metrics being measured. Too often metrics are built at the beginning of a calendar or fiscal year or built around a specific problem and then the business conditions change, yet the metric is still being tracked. This creates both unnecessary effort and disregard for the data. High functioning organizations create a Non-Negotiable Metric Iteration process that happens every 90 days – The intentionality of a 90 Day Review drives teams to ask and answer the question – "Who Cares? Does this Still Matter?" – The intentionality of Iteration is a key driver. Time and again we have seen organizations improve performance every 90 days. This is fundamental to making a Continuous Improvement Culture meaningful and relevant. This is the heart of a PQ culture.

Additionally, throughout the deployment of new processes, continuous monitoring and adjustment is essential. This dynamic management involves gathering real-time data and feedback from users to make informed adjustments that address unanticipated challenges or inefficiencies. Such ongoing evaluations allow leaders to fine-tune processes, ensuring that they not only function optimally but evolve as necessary to meet shifting organizational needs.

When CSI works with clients to bring Process Intelligence to life, we design a "go live" date for the implementation of a new way of measuring metrics and actions. We focus on "metrics that matter" and on helping clients capture the actions in real time, ensuring a common understanding of who is responsible, and the timing of the action.

Clients usually don't "get it right" the first time, and that is to be expected. That is why continuous feedback is so important. After the Go Live date, clients refine their metrics, and their "action register" based on this learning, creating a positive feedback loop that helps drive improved performance.

> Are you visualizing or utilizing data? – High Functioning Leaders recognize it's not about the data, it's about the system of use!

Case Study: Regional Services Corp's Metrics-to-Action Transformation

Regional Services Corp's leaders faced a significant challenge: They had created comprehensive metrics systems with multiple dashboards and reports, but there was a considerable gap in converting these metrics into actionable steps. This disconnect led to limited action on red metrics, inconsistent follow-through on initiatives, and prolonged meetings that yielded low productivity. Without a robust link between metrics and execution, opportunities for improvement were often missed or delayed.

In other words, the strategy was sound but they just couldn't execute it sufficiently.

To address these issues, CSI helped Regional Services Corp to produce a significant change in their execution model, using the concepts of PQ. That change mandated corrective actions tied to any red metric.

Regional established a dynamic review process with clear ownership assignments, so that each corrective action had a designated individual responsible for its execution. They also regularly evaluated the effectiveness of their actions ensuring that efforts were not only initiated but also that they resulted in meaningful outcomes.

Moreover, the company transformed their meeting structures to enhance productivity. As part of the PQ best practices, meetings began with a review of actions, explicitly tying agenda items back to previous discussions and commitments. Specific time allocations were made for action updates, keeping the team focused and meetings concise.

They also implemented Protocols to renegotiate action due dates, which allowed team to adjust plans in a structured manner. Regular accountability assessments made during meetings ensured that all members would uphold their commitments.

Culturally, Regional Services Corp shifted its focus from merely reporting metric outcomes to emphasizing actionable responses. They nurtured an environment that developed problem-solving skills and maintained clear feedback loops. By implementing recognition systems, they also reinforced the importance of completing actions and achieving results, motivating team members to engage more fully and deeply with their responsibilities.

The results of these efforts were substantial and measurable. After one year, the company realized a 65% reduction in "Recurring Quality Issues" – Issues that were thought to be fixed, only to reoccur again over time. This chronic recycling of the same issues pointed to the failure to create "Root Cause Action Plans." Once these Root Cause Action Plans were implemented, the team was able to stop putting short term/bandaid fixes on issues and truly solve repetitive quality issues. Metric response times improved by 45%, demonstrating an increased agility in addressing issues as they arose. A 70% increase in first-time problem resolution was also achieved, reflecting more efficient and effective initial action planning. Additionally, meeting times were cut by an impressive 50%, while action completion rates improved by an outstanding 85%.

Throughout this journey, Regional Services Corp demonstrated the power of connecting business acumen to execution. By embedding accountability into their operations and fostering an action-focused culture, they significantly enhanced their overall operational efficiency and problem-solving capabilities. This transformation underscores the profound impact of turning data insights into decisive, organized actions within any organization.

Similar to Regional Services Corp, 3M faced significant challenges that they overcame with PQ. According to Dr. Rebecca Teeters, President, 3M Chemical Operations, "Having had the privilege of working closely with Shane and the CSI Team over the past decade, I can attest to the transformative impact his insights on leadership have had on my personal journey. Shane's thought processes and methodologies are a masterclass in setting clear goals, engaging and developing people, and implementing systems for repeatable excellence. His approach to building a high-performing leadership culture, centered on the pillars of clarity, connectivity, and consistency, is both practical and inspiring, and it has become my mantra. Shane's guidance has not only refined my leadership style but has also fundamentally improved my team's performance and elevated our business results."

3. System Integration Intelligence

System Integration Intelligence serves as the connective tissue holding an organization's varied processes together, ensuring they function together within the company's broader operations. This requires an in-depth understanding of both new and existing processes along with the technical acumen to integrate them so that data flows efficiently across platforms, and operational bottlenecks are minimized.

What it involves:

- Connecting different systems so data flows efficiently and bottlenecks are minimized
- Making sure systems enhance rather than conflict with each other
- Building bridges between technology and people so systems actually meet daily needs

- Creating organizational ecosystems where everything works together toward common goals and sustainable progress

Note: We know this sounds like there is a huge technical lift to rolling out PQ. We have found this is not the case, through decades of working with clients. There is an IT element of process change and problem solving, but it's not overly complex.

Ensuring that these systems complement rather than conflict is another crucial aspect. Leaders must have an eye for detail and strategy, aligning systems so that they enhance each other's functionality. This involves identifying potential points of friction or overlap and adjusting systems to work together, thereby enhancing overall productivity and efficiency.

Leaders need to facilitate collaboration between IT professionals and end-users, ensuring that technical designs meet practical, day-to-day requirements. This alignment minimizes resistance and enhances user adoption, as systems become intuitive and responsive to the needs of those interacting with them.

The goal is simple, build a workplace where people and technology work well together and help employees solve problems. When your team, your processes, and your technology are all pulling in the same direction, you can solve business challenges flexibly without wasting time or money.

4. Sustainability Intelligence

Sustainability Intelligence is the ability to create organizational systems that can endure and thrive for the long term. It begins with the ability to design for long-term viability. This involves creating processes that not only meet current needs but are flexible and robust enough to evolve with future demands and technological advances.

What it involves:

- Designing for long-term viability with flexibility for future needs
- Building self-correction mechanisms so systems automatically detect and fix problems
- Planning for succession so systems work regardless of personnel changes
- Ensuring knowledge transfer through documentation and training

Making It Simpler

You're building systems that can survive and thrive without you. Like a well-designed building, they're built to last.

As indicated above, sustaining any high-performing organization requires systems and technology. We are obviously fans of our Visuant® software, which is purpose-built to support Process Intelligence. Visuant® combines scorecards, dashboards, meetings, and actions into one place, making it easy for organizations to stay on top of their leadership priorities.

Whether you choose our tool or another set of tools, technology is needed that makes it easy to run meetings, capture actions, and see results quickly and easily. This avoids "data overload" and makes sure that any red metrics get corrective actions ASAP, and not after the meeting concludes.

Digitization Through the Lens of Process Intelligence

Everywhere one turns, organizations are blitzed with data discussions and dilemmas. At CSI, we don't believe the fundamental problem is a lack of data. In fact most organizations have more data than they will ever use or consume. The issue we often see is that the focus becomes on data visualization rather than data utilization. Too often organizations become intoxicated with dynamic charts and graphs and forget the purpose of digitization. It isn't about how pretty the document is, but rather how has the team agreed to utilize the data so that it answers the following questions:

1. Are we winning or losing?
2. Based on that knowledge, do we need to affirm positive performance or take corrective actions for negative performance?
3. Over time, based on historical trends in the data (typically every 90 days) are we iterating the metrics to ensure they are current with content of conversations happening within the organization?

This type of utilization process creates a culture of players, not spectators. Too often when an organization digitizes without a utilization process, the outcome becomes better visualization, but sadly the engagement can be engineered out of the process. High functioning organizations recognize they have to implement visualization tools, but coupled with those visualization tools must be a robust utilization process that educates, facilitates, and iterates the metrics so that the output is a highly engaged culture of players not sepectators.

Core Principles of Process Intelligence

Several key principles guide the development and application of Process Intelligence:

1. The System Principle

"What works must be systematized; what is systematized must work."

The System Principle highlights the importance of capturing and structuring effective processes within reliable systems. This principle underscores two key components: the documentation of successful methods and the assurance of their effectiveness.

To start, any process that is working well should be documented and built into a formal system, so it can be replicated.

Yet, creating documentation is not solely about documentation; it also requires that these systems consistently deliver desired results. Keep monitoring and improving your systems over time.

By integrating thorough documentation with ongoing evaluation, the System Principle aims to achieve a balance between structure and adaptability, promoting a culture of reliability and continuous improvement in organizational processes.

2. The Scalability Principle

"Every solution must be designed with growth in mind."

Think about how your processes and solutions will work when your organization is twice as large as it is today. Build systems that can handle increased workloads and complexity without breaking down.

A scalable system should accommodate growth smoothly, ensuring that its performance remains reliable as the organization's needs evolve. This means designing processes and systems that can handle increased workloads, user additions, or expanded functionalities without losing effectiveness or efficiency.

By ingraining scalability into the design phase, organizations can foster resilience and adaptability, positioning themselves to effectively manage growth and capitalize on new opportunities as they arise.

As we pointed out earlier, building processes for scalability is challenging at the outset. That's why we often see clients iterate their way to success.

3. The Sustainability Principle
"Systems should outlive their creators."

It's important to design processes that will work regardless of who is running them. As we have seen with the US Army Organic Industrial Base of 23 Depots, Arsenals, and Ammunition Plants, changing the Commander of the Depot every two years doesn't change their "way of work." The leadership systems that have been developed are sustainable and drive peak performance.

Document everything thoroughly to ensure that knowledge of how things operate is not tied to specific individuals. This involves creating comprehensive guides and resources that allow new team members to understand and manage processes seamlessly.

Moreover, sustainability requires systems to be adaptable, capable of accommodating shifts in technology, market conditions, and organizational needs. This adaptability ensures that systems remain effective and pertinent, even as the environment in which they operate evolves.

By prioritizing sustainability in the design and implementation of processes, organizations can safeguard their operations against disruptions and ensure continuity, stability, and ongoing success, no matter who is at the helm.

"As a participant in the Army's Organic Industrial Base Leadership Course, customer to CSI's Process Based Leadership®, and a personal mentee, the relationship with Shane and the CSI team is forged through through a shared vision, aligned thinking, and doing what is right for both the business and our people. CSI's processes and methodologies have brought my organization of more than 600 people and operating revenue of $400M to new heights. CSI has taught us how to move from transactional operations to generational transformation. That mindset has shaped how we lead, how we adapt, and how we grow—turning complexity into opportunity and fostering resilience at every level of the business. We have driven the business forward financially, modernized our systems and infrastructure, and developed our workforce by leaps and bounds since we partnered with the CSI Team. Shane is a transformational leader and radiates those qualities in all his interactions. We are forever indebted to him for his leadership."

—Anthony Fabrizio
Deputy Commander

4. The Integration Principle
"Systems must connect, not conflict."

For systems to integrate effectively, they must be designed with a holistic perspective in mind. This involves considering how each system interacts with others, ensuring that data flows effortlessly and activities are synchronized across the organization. Such integration minimizes redundancy, reduces operational friction, and enhances overall efficiency.

Additionally, successful integration requires ongoing communication and collaboration across departments to align objectives and understand interdependencies. This collaborative approach helps conflicts to be avoided, and it leverages synergies, thereby enabling systems to complement each other and support broader organizational goals.

While this might sound difficult or complex, it doesn't have to be. Many of our clients utilize a "pass up / pass down" principle to get important information flowing upward and downward in an organization. *The key here is that pass-ups and pass-downs are not just emails. They are embedded into a meeting design, so they can be acted on. Email notifications are ignored way too often ("I didn't see that").*

By adhering to the Integration Principle, organizations can create a cohesive operational environment where every component works in concert, enhancing effectiveness and driving unified progress.

Developing Process Intelligence

Unlike IQ, which is relatively fixed, and EQ, which develops through personal growth, PQ can be systematically developed through specific practices and approaches:

Process Design

Process Design involves structuring and optimizing organizational workflows to enhance efficiency and effectiveness.

Arrange tasks and activities in a sequence that minimizes waste and reduces bottlenecks. Analyze existing processes to streamline steps, integrate automation where possible, and ensure that resources are optimally allocated.

Implement checkpoints or data collection points where performance can be assessed and adjustments made based on real-time insights, ensuring processes remain aligned with organizational goals.

Anticipate future needs and incorporate flexible structures that allow processes to expand or adapt smoothly, ensuring that systems remain robust and efficient as the organization evolves.

Implementation Planning

Implementation Planning is the phase in which ideas get put into action, setting the foundation for successful new initiatives. Develop rollout strategies, including clear timelines, assign responsibilities, and ensure that all logistical aspects align to ensure a smooth transition.

Appropriate training is vital to equip team members with the necessary skills and knowledge to effectively work within the new framework. With the right training, organizations can minimize resistance and maximize the adoption of new processes, thus ensuring that everyone is on the same page from the start.

Finally, make sure you know how to measure performance. By measuring outcomes, organizations can gather valuable data, make informed adjustments, and continuously refine processes to ensure they meet desired objectives.

Process Maintenance

Continuously monitor how well your systems are working. Make systematic improvements from the insights you gather from your monitoring. Targeted enhancements will improve performance and align the system with the organization's evolving needs.

The PQ Advantage: Breaking Free from Traditional Limitations

Process Intelligence offers several distinct advantages that address the limitations of traditional leadership approaches:

Scalability Without Sacrifice

One of the most striking benefits of PQ is its ability to support an organization's growth without compromising on quality. As companies expand, maintaining the qualities that contributed to their initial success can become a significant challenge. PQ addresses this by systematizing best practices across the board, ensuring consistency and quality remain intact as operations scale and new processes are introduced. This strategic implementation allows organizations to grow their reach and capabilities while staying true to their core values and standards, preventing dilution of excellence during expansion.

Sustainability Beyond Individual Leaders

Traditional leadership approaches often place significant dependency on charismatic leaders or key individuals, which can create vulnerabilities during transitions. The shift to PQ means that the organization is no longer tied to the strengths of a few individuals. Leadership changes become seamless, as the significant knowledge and practices are institutionalized, fostering a culture where the organization thrives beyond the influence or presence of any single leader.

Case Study: Global Services International - The EQ-PQ Integration

Global Services International (GSI) found itself grappling with a challenge that seemed paradoxical. Despite having leaders endowed with strong business acumen and high emotional intelligence, GSI was unable to consistently harness these capabilities to create organizational success. Recognizing this disconnect, GSI embarked on a transformative journey that highlighted the synergies achieved by integrating Emotional Intelligence (EQ) with Process Intelligence (PQ).

GSI knew, having benchmarked many of their peers, that their organization was strong. They possessed a solid Talent Recruitment Team who took screening and qualifying potential candidates very seriously. Finding, hiring, and retaining smart people was a personal passion of the Talent Recruitment Team Leader. Once a candidate accepted an offer and began employment, they were immediately enrolled in the GSI's Employee Development program. This program was sponsored by the Learning & Development organization and represented a six-month immersion into the principles of Emotional Intelligence (EQ). GSI truly believed that if Talent Recruitment could hire smart people, they could certainly mold them into compassionate, EQ centered employees. GSI followed this approach religiously and in doing so churned out strong IQ/EQ leaders. But cracks were developing in both functional performance and cross functional execution. Patterns emerged where teams wanted the same key individuals on every team and in every project. Recognizing this wasn't sustainable, GSI engaged an outside consulting firm to try to discover why the same key individuals were highly sought after as key drivers within the GSI organization. As the consulting firm began to assess the GSI culture some dramatic findings began to emerge.

#1 – The coveted GSI colleagues possessed a series of attributes not found in the broader GSI organization. While they were recruited with the same IQ and EQ focus, they had brought with them a skill set from a previous employer – System Thinking.

#2 – System Thinking is the principle that to truly fix a problem, the solution must be grounded in a visible, codified, repeatable process that is understood by every member of the team.

#3 – To create a visible, codified, repeatable process, ideally the team should be the authors of that process so there is broad buy-in and support of the defined systems. Too often, organizations adopt an "off the shelf" mentality that if a process/system worked in another organization, its as simple as cherry picking the elements that apply and rebranding the initiative to fit their culture. This "off the shelf" systemic design never gets traction because there is no pride of ownership.

After 18 months of implementing these integrated systems, GSI saw significant positive changes. Customer satisfaction scores rose by 45%, reflecting the company's enhanced ability to understand and respond to customer needs. Client churn, a crucial metric for assessing service continuity and satisfaction, dropped by 35%, illustrating the effectiveness of the improved relationship management and communication strategies. Additionally, cross-selling success increased by 60%, pointing to better comprehension of client needs and opportunities for additional services. Employee engagement, a vital component of sustained organizational performance, improved by 40%, underlining the positive impact of a more coherent and supportive operational environment.

GSI's journey underscores the powerful potential of integrating EQ with PQ. This case highlights not only how emotional intelligence can be grounded and multiplied through Process Intelligence but also how this integration can lead to substantial improvements in both client-facing and internal metrics.

Predictable Performance

In the realm of traditional methods, variability in outcomes is a common issue due to differing leadership styles and decision-making processes. PQ changes this by implementing systematic approaches to navigate challenges, resulting in more consistent and predictable results. This empowers organizations to better anticipate outcomes, refine strategies, and to allocate resources more effectively, leading to enhanced performance and stability in operations.

By enabling leaders to see issues immediately as they emerge through the use of scorecards and metrics, PQ enables early intervention to head off looming problems. Furthermore, PQ creates accountability and visibility for solutions to those problems.

Improved Adaptability

A huge advantage of PQ is its ability to increase organizational adaptability. While systematic approaches might seem confining at first glance, they actually provide a robust framework for managing change. This clarity and order enable organizations to adapt more efficiently to shifts in the marketplace or internal environments, ensuring they remain responsive and agile. With PQ, organizations can implement changes rapidly and with confidence, leveraging structured systems to embrace change rather than resist it.

This is underscored by what Edward DuBeau, SVP & Global Business Lead of the NextGen ERP Program at Zoetis said, "The enduring power of CSI's mantra—consistency and clarity—has enabled colleagues at all levels of my organization to become truly aligned and connected. Over the years, Shane and the CSI Team has imparted some of the most valuable leadership and life lessons I've ever received, centered on the delicate balance between accountability and personal empathy. Ironically, while Shane consistently drives teams to focus on their operating metrics, the true impact he has had in transforming these teams and organizations is immeasurable. From the very first leadership project kick-off meeting to the ongoing daily shift huddles, CSI's systems serve as a powerful performance multiplier. Beyond being a highly trusted thought partner, Shane is, most importantly, a genuine friend."

Conclusion

As we've explored throughout this chapter, Process Intelligence is not just another leadership skill. It's the critical missing link that can enable leaders of organizations to fully leverage both IQ and EQ. By completing the Leadership Triangle, PQ transforms individual capability into organizational capacity, personal influence into systematic impact, and temporary success into sustainable excellence.

In the chapters that follow, we will explore specific strategies for developing PQ in leaders and organizations, we will examine case studies of successful PQ implementation, and we will provide practical tools for building a PQ.

WORKBOOK

Process Intelligence (PQ) Status

Rate you or your company on a scale of 1 (Strongly Disagree) to 5 (Strongly Agree) for each statement.

Imagine you're faced with a challenge at work:

1. IQ approach, "I know how to solve this problem." ___

2. EQ perspective, "I can help people work together to solve this problem." ___

3. PQ perspective, "I can create a system that enables people to solve similar problems consistently." ___

Growing businesses need leaders who can scale. In my company:

1. Knowledge often ends up trapped within the minds of experts. ___

2. Processes and capabilities are hindered by the absence of key individuals. ___

3. Leaders facilitate collaboration between IT professionals and end-users. ___

4. Systems are built that can handle increased workloads and complexity without breaking down. ___

5. Processes are built that will work regardless of who is running them. ___

6. Tasks and activities are arranged in a sequence that minimizes waste and reduces bottlenecks. ___

Reflection:

1 Which area needs the most development?

2. What specific actions can you take to improve your weakest area?

Part Two:

Business Acumen Process
Execution Process
Communication Process
Ideal Behavior Process

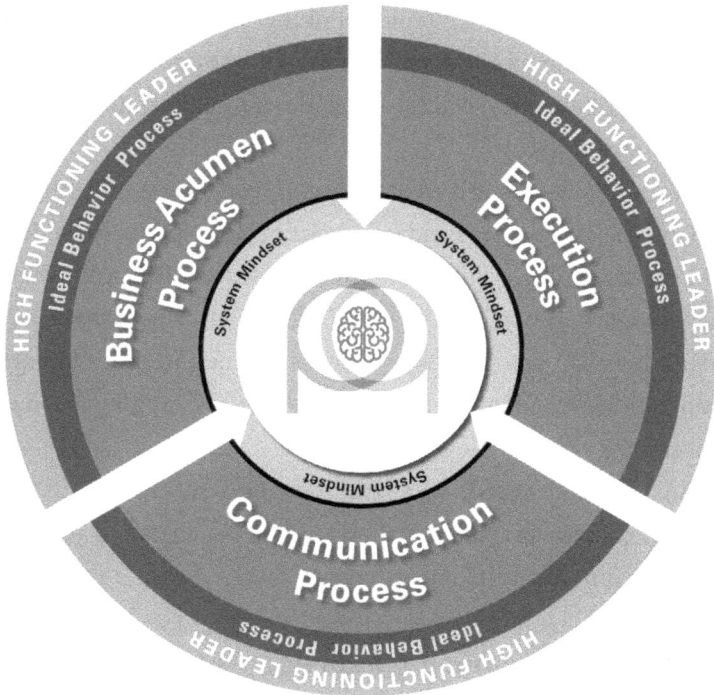

Chapter Five

Business Acumen Process
"Are We Winning or Losing?"

Chapter Five shifts focus to a key application of PQ: the enhancement and arrangement of business acumen into a process. Business acumen is more than just an intuitive grasp of strategic decision-making, it is a skill that can improve an organization's strategic intelligence so that it becomes part of its very fabric.

PQ ensures that strategic thinking does not remain the exclusive domain of a few individuals, but rather, that it becomes a shared competency that will guide an organization toward sustainable success.

Through process-driven strategies, leaders can demystify the decision-making process and enable teams to effectively embrace and execute strategic initiatives. In other words, PQ provides the key linkage between strategy and execution. This chapter will explain how PQ can improve business acumen in order to equip organizations to adapt and thrive in an ever-changing business landscape.

As you read ahead, you will learn how to embed strategic intelligence into the organization's DNA to ensure a resilient, agile, and forward-thinking enterprise.

The Business Acumen Challenge: Integrating IQ, EQ, and PQ

Business acumen has often mistakenly been confused as being an extension of intelligence, a field reserved for those with high IQs who can decode the intricate language of numbers and strategy. However, looking more deeply into this reveals that effective business acumen can emerge from the implementation of a triad of disciplines: IQ, EQ, and PQ. Each can make a distinct contribution that when combined can form the bedrock of a resilient, forward-thinking organization.

The IQ Component: Analytical Mastery

The traditional IQ component is at the forefront of this combination. It employs business metrics and financial data to harness analytical data and not only crunches numbers but also interprets them in a way that informs strategic thinking and problem-solving. Leaders with this capability are able to delve into market and competitive analyses to predict trends and craft data-driven strategies.

Moreover, the prowess to analyze data extends beyond immediate business metrics, enabling leaders to investigate broad economic terrain in order to anticipate shifts. This gives those with a high level of intellectual curiosity the ability to leverage information, which is indispensable for strategic forecasting.

The EQ Component: Emotional Intelligence in Action

EQ complements the analytical component by infusing business acumen with a human touch. Understanding stakeholder needs and motivations, for example, can be pivotal, and EQ makes it possible for the organization's operatives to transcend simple transactions in order to form lasting relationships. Those with high EQ can also read and respond to market sentiment. This allows them to adjust strategies so that they align with public perceptions and evolving consumer demands.

Building trust with customers and partners is not only an interpersonal skill, it is a strategic imperative. By enabling the cultivation of complex relationships across organizational and cultural boundaries, EQ promotes resilience and adaptability in leadership—qualities required for success in today's rapidly evolving business environment.

The PQ Component: Integration and Execution

Process Intelligence is integral to the evolution of business acumen. It serves as a linchpin for scaling intelligence throughout an organization. PQ is used to create robust systems that capture and disseminate comprehensive business data and information. By making use of this in-depth intelligence when decisions are being made, leaders ensure that an organization's strategies are not just innovative, but that they are easily executed, and that results can be measured and quantified.

PQ helps you put clear frameworks and repeatable processes in place so your strategies are carried out consistently across the company. It also makes sure that the wisdom from both IQ and EQ of your people are shared and used in a way that benefits everyone. Just as important, PQ adds ways for the organization to keep learning and adapting—so you can grow and improve based on real-world results and feedback.

An organization may have senior leaders with exceptional business acumen, but such valuable expertise often remains confined to them rather than being integrated into the organization's systems. Sequestered knowledge leads to several problems. Decision-making may suffer from bottlenecks, as key insights are accessible only to a select few, which of course slows down the organization's ability to respond quickly and effectively to changing circumstances, which not unexpectedly creates challenging situations,

In addition, the lack of embedded strategic knowledge almost always results in departments that struggle to consistently align with the organization's goals, thereby causing disjointed efforts and a fragmented focus overall. Moreover, the lack of embedded strategic knowledge makes it difficult if not impossible to scale business intelligence across the organization, thereby hindering the ability to fully harness the power of data-driven strategies and informed decision-making across all levels.

The development of future leaders also suffers, as they miss out on opportunities to engage with and build upon strategic insights. This leaves organizations vulnerable during leadership transitions because the departure of key leaders can strip the organization of critical expertise, threatening stability and continuity.

Addressing these challenges requires more than simply training individuals in business acumen. The solution lies in creating processes that embed business intelligence throughout an organization. By doing so, strategic insights are transformed from individual assets into an integral part of the fabric of the organization, thus empowering all members to contribute to and benefit from a shared bank of knowledge while ensuring long-term resilience and growth.

The Process Intelligence Approach to Business Acumen

"Are we winning or losing?" That's the question to ask if you want to know how effective the business acumen is and how well it is being employed. Despite sophisticated data analytics, reporting tools, dashboards, and metrics, many organizations struggle to answer this question clearly and concisely. The PQ process of Business Acumen is designed specifically to create a system that allows this fundamental question to be answered in a clear, meaningful, and actionable manner.

Process Intelligence transforms business acumen from the purview of certain individuals into an organization via three key components:

Goal Setting and Alignment

In many organizations, goals and their alignment across the organization is left to a combination of different individuals. This can and often does result in misalignment and fragmented focus. PQ leaders, however, implement structured processes that leave no room for ambiguity. They start by identifying Key Business Focus Areas (KBFAs), which set the stage for aligning departmental goals with the overarching organizational strategy.

This alignment is then cascaded throughout the entire organization, thus ensuring that each individual and each team understands its specific role in achieving the articulated goals. By establishing a clear accountability framework, PQ leaders ensure every layer of the organization is moving in concert toward the same objectives with focus and precision.

Dynamic Business Scorecards

Traditional scorecards typically offer limited utility for driving future actions because they are static snapshots of past performance. Organizations employing Process Intelligence revolutionize such tools by transforming them into dynamic management systems that communicate in a standardized business language everyone understands, thereby ensuring clarity and consistency in performance evaluation across the board.

The result is that dynamic PQ scorecards connect individual actions directly to broader organizational outcomes in order to drive real-time decision-making. This coupling facilitates not only proactive performance management, it allows for immediate corrective actions that keep the organization responsive to market shifts and demands.

Integrated Feedback Loops

High-PQ organizations excel in establishing robust feedback mechanisms that capture crucial business intelligence. These are designed to distribute insights across an organization rapidly in order to enable swift adaptation to changes occurring externally as well as internally.

However, feedback loops do not exist solely for reactive purposes. They drive organizational learning and foster a culture of continuous improvement that results in significant benefits. By integrating feedback into everyday operations, High-PQ organizations have an enhanced ability to adapt and innovate, giving them a competitive advantage in environments that are undergoing rapid change.

The Business Acumen Process System

Component 1: Strategic Framework

The cornerstone of the Business Acumen Process is its clearly defined strategic framework, which is integral to steering an organization towards its goals. This framework includes six Key Business Focus Areas (KBFAs): quality, cost, safety, productivity, people, and customer service. The framework deploys a shared language and a uniform structure across an organization to ensure that front-line employees all the way to those at the top are able to fully comprehend the state of each focus area at all times.

Rather than rely on anecdotal information rooted in feelings, attitudes, and biases that can be and often are misleading, metrics based on empirical data are used to guide those involved. Such data is supported by robust processes for education, facilitation, and iteration, ensuring that metrics not only inform but that in addition to day-to-day decision-making, they actively guide the improvements made on an ongoing basis.

The approach to visualizing data differs significantly from low-functioning organizations, the personnel of which often experience visualization overload because of busy and excessive scorecards and dashboards that foster a passive, "spectator culture." In contrast, high-functioning organizations employ a process that ensures that metrics are meaningful and actionable as well as underpinned by educational and facilitative efforts.

In terms of reporting, low-functioning organizations exhibit a thermometer approach, simply reporting data without instigating change. Conversely, high-functioning organizations employ a thermostat approach, enabling dynamic actions and adjustments based on robust data insights.

Lastly, the focus on explanation versus execution highlights another vital distinction. Low-functioning organizations may prioritize storytelling around data without implementing corrective actions. High-functioning organizations focus on execution by following clear processes that address issues and implement solutions, thereby translating data insights into effective organizational practices.

Component 2: A Dynamic Business Scorecard

Too often organizations see metrics as a calendar-driven activity where each team in an organization has until the end of January, for example, to set their targets for the calendar year. Once this has been done, the task feels completed. Unfortunately, this is often the manifestation of a "thermometer" mindset, i.e., the metrics are set, so we are done.

Typically, critical focus areas change, markets move, demands change, and suddenly, the metrics that were thought to be important on January 15th are no longer meaningful. The content of the conversation changed, but the metrics didn't. A team might go into their weekly meeting with their metrics projected on a screen. They will fill five minutes discussing metrics that are no longer drivers of the business, and feel like they need to review these metrics, because that is the process. The metrics, and the meeting itself, aren't driving action, urgency, collaboration, or accountability. The metrics have become passive reports built around data that seemed meaningful but now feel stale and irrelevant.

This is the opposite of a "Thermostatic" approach in which teams are acting on metrics every week. Using this approach, the team will build a regular metric review process during which they will look at past performance and ask a very simple question, "Who cares about this metric? Who cares about the color of performance? Does this metric really move our business forward?" These are alignment questions that gauge if the metric is aligned with the purpose of the meeting. When those two things align, a rich, timely, and relevant conversation takes place. When not aligned, businesses can feel like there is a "hidden factory" generating charts and graphs that nobody cares about.

To keep metrics and actions regularly aligned, CSI developed Visuant®, software that combines metric management (scorecards and dashboards), action registers, and meeting management in one tool. Most companies use software scorecards as static thermometers, simply recording data without fostering change. Visuant® enables businesses not only to measure performance but also to instigate change, highlighting the scorecard's pivotal role in driving action rather than merely reporting status.

Central to Visuant's® effectiveness is the integration to ensure a seamless connection between strategic goals and tactical measures. By fostering cross-functional alignment, the software ensures that each department's actions contribute meaningfully to the organization's overarching objectives. Real-time performance indicators are embedded within the scorecard, equipping leaders with the timely insights needed to respond swiftly to shifting conditions and emerging challenges.

When companies utilize SMART objectives, goals that are Specific, Measurable, Achievable, Relevant, and Time-bound, that further strengthen the benefit of their scorecard review. This approach brings clarity and precision to goal-setting, providing a robust foundation for evaluating progress. It ensures that every objective is not only aligned with broader strategies but also adaptable to changing business landscapes in order to maintain focus and direction.

The use of Visuant®, or a similar tool that closely aligns metrics and actions, helps maintain clear ownership and accountability. Specific individuals are designated as metric owners tasked with the responsibility of tracking and reporting on the performance areas they have been assigned. Through its comprehensive approach, the tight linkage provided by Visuant® transforms business metrics into powerful tools for action and adaptation.

Further, high-functioning organizations utilize regular review cycles to evaluate and adapt metrics and actions to link strategy and execution, closing the loop between data collection, data review, and strategic execution.

"Visuant® has become an essential data analytics tool for Rust-oleum, allowing us to easily track and view our metric performance across the enterprise. The direct linkage of corrective actions to underperforming metrics has driven a heightened level of execution and accountability within our meetings and throughout our facilities. Most importantly, it has driven bottom line improvements in a hypercompetitive operational landscape."

Brian Vance
Senior Manager Continuous Improvement

∷RUST-OLEUM

Component 3: The Review Process

The backbone of the Business Acumen Process is the Review Process that incorporates structured mechanisms that ensure continuous improvement and alignment with strategic objectives. This component is designed to provide organizations with a disciplined approach to performance evaluation and strategic recalibration.

Daily Performance Dialogue initiates this ongoing process with quick but effective performance checks that identify potential problems and issues as they arise. These daily dialogues are essential in that they allow for immediate intervention through rapid response protocols. This approach ensures that minor problems are addressed promptly thereby preventing them from escalating into larger issues.

Complementing the daily checks are Weekly Strategic Reviews, which offer a broader perspective on organizational performance. These reviews focus on evaluating progress vis a vis established SMART objectives in order to ensure that all actions are aligned with the strategic vision for the organization. By fostering cross-functional coordination, these weekly evaluations optimize organizational performance and efficiency by facilitating informed resource allocation decisions.

The scorecard review process culminates in Monthly Business Reviews that provide a more comprehensive analysis of trends and strategic outcomes. During these reviews, leaders conduct in-depth trend analyses in order to spot the need for strategic adjustments when and where they might be called for. This part of the process also involves evaluating the overall effectiveness of the system itself to ensure that all components of the Business Acumen Process are functioning optimally.

Through its structured review mechanisms, the scorecard review process enables the organization to maintain a consistent focus on performance and strategic alignment. By integrating daily, weekly, and monthly evaluations, the process ensures that organizations are nimble, responsive, and capable of adapting to both immediate challenges and long-term strategic shifts.

The PQ Metrics Utilization Process

In high-functioning organizations, the PQ Metrics Utilization Process transforms metrics from mere numbers into powerful tools built to lead a business to success. The process involves three key stages: Educate, Facilitate, and Iterate. Each is designed to ensure metrics are not just understood, but that each is used actively to drive meaningful progress.

The first stage, **"Educate,"** focuses on fostering understanding among team members concerning what metrics mean and their importance. It is essential to make clear where the metrics come from and to articulate their significance to the goals of the organization. Doing so ensures that every member appreciates their relevance to the business's strategic objectives.

Moving into the **"Facilitate"** stage, high-functioning organizations restructure meetings with the goal of "Moving the Business Forward." This includes populating metrics in advance and allowing them to guide the meeting's agenda. Data from the metrics helps set the tone, duration, and urgency of discussions, ensuring a meeting is focused and productive. Rather than mere discussions, meetings need to become actionable sessions where metrics drive both the recognition of achievements and the initiation of corrective actions.

The third stage, **"Iterate,"** involves conducting metric reconciliation every 90 days. This periodic review prompts the provocative question, "So What?" and "Who Cares?" for each metric and should elicit critical reflection on the metric's impact. These periodic reviews will drive necessary adjustments and refinements of metrics to make sure they relevant and effective in moving the business forward.

Through this structured process, organizations shift team members from being passive spectators of data into active players who use metrics to propel a business forward to success. As the adage goes, "Players know the score—if you don't know the score, you aren't a player." This truth underscores the value and necessity of this process. When they are clearly understood, and iterative refinement takes place, metrics become central to enabling transformative decision-making and strategic advancement.

Implementation Framework

To successfully implement the Business Acumen Process, organizations should follow these steps:

Phase 1: Foundation Building

In the Foundation Building phase, the organization begins by identifying and defining the Key Business Focus Areas (KBFAs). This is critical as these areas reflect the organization's strategic priorities and should serve as guides to determine how resources and efforts should be allocated. Defining these areas will enable their alignment with the overall business goals and set a clear direction for the process.

Once KBFAs are established, the next step is to create standardized scorecard templates. These templates provide a consistent framework for measuring and tracking performance across different business units and teams and ensure that everyone is focused on the same critical metrics. Establishing review protocols is essential, as they determine the methods and frequency of metric evaluation so that the insights gathered are timely and actionable.

Training process owners is the final step in this phase, as these individuals are pivotal in managing the implementation. Arming them with the necessary skills and knowledge will enable them to lead the process effectively and to troubleshoot any issues that arise.

Phase 2: Rollout

The Rollout phase builds upon the groundwork laid in the first phase and extends it throughout the organization. This begins with cascading the scorecards across all relevant departments and teams and making sure that everyone involved in executing the business strategy has access to the necessary metrics.

It is crucial during this phase to implement regular review cycles, which serve to keep the organization on track. These review cycles also facilitate timely adjustments to strategies and approaches based on the latest data. Monitoring adoption and compliance is a key focus at this stage. It's important to ensure that the new processes are being used as intended and that all team members are adhering to the established protocols.

Gathering feedback is an integral part of this phase as well. Those implementing the process should collect insights from users to find out what is working well and what might need improvement. This should be an ongoing dialogue that helps refine the process while ensuring that it meets the needs of all stakeholders.

Phase 3: Sustainability

The final phase, Sustainability, is about ensuring the longevity and effectiveness of the Business Acumen Process. Regular audits need to be conducted to evaluate whether the process continues to align with the organization's strategic goals and if it remains effective in driving performance.

Continuous improvement mechanisms are crucial for fostering a culture of ongoing growth, enhancement, and refinement so that the process can adapt to internal changes and external market conditions. In addition, leadership development integration ensures that emerging leaders are well-versed in using the Business Acumen Process, enabling them to champion its usage and benefits.

Developing protocols for knowledge transfer is also important in order to maintain consistency and understanding across the organization. This involves creating documentation and instituting training programs so that new employees and other stakeholders can quickly get up to speed with the process.

Case Studies in Process Intelligence Business Acumen

Case Study: Detroit-Based Automotive Supplier (DBAS) Building Systematic Business Intelligence

DBAS Automotive encountered a significant challenge despite having sophisticated data systems and dashboards at the disposal of its leaders. They struggled to answer the fundamental question concerning whether or not they were "winning or losing." This inability stemmed from multiple conflicting scorecard systems and an overwhelming amount of data that did not provide even minimal actionable insights. Moreover, a lack of consistency in metrics across departments compounded the issue, and heavy reliance on individual managers' interpretations added to it.

Faced with this situation, DBAS Automotive leaders embarked on the implementation of a Process Intelligence approach to business acumen in an effort to create coherence and clarity throughout the organization. The initial effort focused on establishing standardized Key Business Focus Areas (KBFAs) that aligned with the company's strategic goals and provided a unified direction for all departments.

The introduction of digital scorecards with real-time updates revolutionized their data interpretation capability, thereby making more immediate and impactful decision-making possible. Tiered daily management systems were put in place alongside this that ensured goals and performance metrics were consistently communicated and reviewed throughout the organization. This led to the creation of systematic review processes that emphasized structured assessments and corrective actions.

The transformation of metrics was a key aspect of this journey. By moving from a passive "thermometer" approach to an active "thermostat" methodology, the company enabled timely interventions and adjustments when data flagged anomalies or inefficiencies. Clear ownership and accountability systems were established, which meant that every team member in each department understood his or her role in executing corrective action protocols. Regular metric reconciliation meetings ensured that everyone was aligned and that discrepancies were swiftly addressed.

Culturally, the organization shifted from a "spectator" mentality, i.e.., employees merely observing metrics, to a "player" mindset in which they actively engaged with and leveraged the data to drive performance. They developed clear processes for educating employees about metrics, completely transforming how they utilized performance data.

This educational framework was part of a broader systematic approach to performance dialogue, which fostered open discussions about goals, outcomes, and improvements. The creation of frameworks for continuous improvement ingrained a culture of ongoing enhancement and adaptation.

The results of this systematic shift became evident after one year. The organization saw a 30% improvement in strategic alignment scores, indicating that all levels were more in tune with the overarching goals. Decision-making cycle time was cut by 25%, reflecting faster and more effective responses to challenges. Employee understanding of business metrics surged by 40%, dramatically increasing the workforce's ability to contribute to the organization's success. Performance variation across shifts was reduced by 50%, ensuring more consistent outcomes. Finally, there was a 35% improvement in the completion rates of corrective actions, demonstrating a more proactive and effective approach to addressing issues. DBAS Automotive's transformation illustrates the profound impacts that a Process Intelligence approach to business intelligence can have on organizational performance and culture.

Key Learning: This success came not from better metrics or more sophisticated dashboards, but rather, it came from creating systematic processes that transformed how metrics were understood, utilized, and acted upon throughout the organization.

Case Study: Regional Healthcare Network - Metrics That Matter

Regional Healthcare Network (RHN) provides a powerful example of how Process Intelligence can be leveraged to transform business acumen within a complex service-oriented environment. Initially, RHN faced several challenges that impeded the ability to deliver consistent service across the organization's various facilities. Diverse departments were using different performance metrics, complicating the ability to link daily operations and strategic objectives. As a result, performance was inconsistent from one facility to another, and the organization struggled to implement improvements across the company.

Faced with these challenges, RHN embarked on a comprehensive implementation approach, starting with metrics. They reduced the total number of metrics from over 150 down to 40 critical indicators—key metrics that directly supported their strategic goals. Moreover, a clear hierarchy of metrics was established that linked operational measures to strategic objectives to streamline the focus across the organization. Additionally, a systematic metric review process was implemented to maintain metric relevance and alignment with organizational goals.

To further enhance this transformation, they worked hard to standardize processes. Consistent performance dialogue frameworks were developed to ensure that performance discussions were structured and productive. They implemented a consistent approach to problem-solving by creating a consistent way of handling metric variations. The organization also implemented cross-facility performance calibration to ensure that all facilities were aligned and operating at similar performance levels. They created a knowledge-sharing process to help adopt best practices across the network.

They integrated these changes deeply into their culture. Leaders received training on Process Based Leadership® to equip them to champion these new methodologies. Ownership was established for each metric to create a sense of accountability, responsibility, and empowerment among staff. Regular forums were created to review metrics in order to foster an environment of continual improvement. They also developed coaching processes to support leaders and teams, ensuring ongoing development and optimization of processes.

After 15 months, the results were striking. RHN achieved a 45% reduction in metric reporting time, which indicated the significantly streamlined data management process. First-time issue resolution improved by 60%, demonstrating the greatly enhanced quality and efficiency of the care provided. Employee

From our earliest meeting, my professional relationship with Shane Yount and Competitive Solutions, Inc (CSI) has been a model of trust, respect, and shared purpose. Their approach to business leadership has not only catalyzed remarkable transformation within the organizations I have led but has also profoundly influenced my own outlook as a leader. By introducing us to methodologies that prioritize transparency, continuous improvement, and robust engagement at every level, they have enabled us to cultivate environments where accountability is not just a word, but a lived value. This shift has been transformative. Our teams, once plagued by uncertainty over goals and expectations, are now unified by clear metrics, shared priorities, and a collective sense of ownership. The ripple effects of this clarity have extended far beyond improved performance indicators—they have fostered a culture of mutual respect, candor, and relentless pursuit of excellence. Over the years, I have come to regard our partnership as a source of inspiration and a benchmark for excellence in organizational effectiveness. I can say with complete confidence that our relationship with Competitive Solutions has been among the most positive, productive, and rewarding of my career. Their practical methodologies have not only delivered concrete results but have also left an indelible mark on the way I lead and the cultures I strive to cultivate.

Frank R. Hacker,
Vice President Manufacturing

rockline
people who make it right

engagement scores increased by 35%, which was indicative of greater alignment and motivation among staff. Performance variation between facilities was reduced by 28%, indicating more consistent service delivery. Finally, strategic goal achievement saw a 40% improvement, which serves to underscore the success of the metric-driven approach.

Key Learning: Success came not simply from simplifying metrics, but from creating processes that made metrics meaningful and actionable at every level of the organization.

Integrating IQ, EQ, and PQ in Business Acumen Development

The key to developing sustainable business acumen lies in understanding how IQ, EQ, and PQ work together:

From Individual to Organizational Intelligence

The journey begins with IQ, which lays the analytical groundwork necessary for understanding complexities and making informed decisions. It is through IQ that organizations derive insights from data, setting the stage for strategic thinking and problem-solving. However, translating analytical prowess into action requires EQ, which facilitates the effective application of IQ insights. EQ allows leaders to connect with teams and stakeholders, ensuring that decisions resonate with those they impact. PQ, on the other hand, plays a critical role in systematically distributing and scaling intelligence across the organization. By creating processes that embed insights into daily operations, PQ ensures that intelligence is not confined to a few individuals but becomes a collective asset.

Building Sustainable Capabilities

To build capabilities that endure, each element of the IQ-EQ-PQ triad must function with the others seamlessly. IQ gives leaders the insight to identify which are the crucial metrics to be tracked that ultimately can be improved if and when the need arises. EQ is used to determine how to engage people with these metrics and the actions needed to improve them by fostering an environment in which team members feel connected to act on insights rather than simply sitting back and observing them. PQ rounds out the effort by automating processes that ensure consistent execution. PQ ties strategic intent to execution enabling intentions to be transformed into tangible results.

Ensuring Consistent Performance

Achieving consistency in performance is essential for success. IQ plays a pivotal role by defining clear success criteria by identifying the benchmarks against which performance is to be measured. EQ contributes by maintaining engagement and securing buy-in from stakeholders, thereby ensuring that everyone remains committed to the organization's goals. PQ establishes mechanisms that guarantee reliable delivery by creating pathways that ensure every team and individual can meet the defined success criteria with confidence and efficiency.

Enabling Organizational Learning

Finally, the integration of IQ, EQ, and PQ fosters a learning culture. IQ helps leaders capture key insights from data and experiences, forming the knowledge base from which learning occurs. EQ facilitates the effective sharing of this knowledge by building relationships and communication so ideas and insights flow freely among teams. PQ creates systems to measure results, and to track team and individual actions so that learning is not only disseminated but also institutionalized within the organization. By doing so, organizations can continuously adapt and evolve, turning knowledge into a persistent and ongoing competitive advantage.

The Future of Business Acumen

As organizations continue to evolve in an increasingly complex business environment, the integration of IQ, EQ, and PQ in business acumen becomes even more critical. Future leaders must not only possess strong business acumen for themselves personally, they must also be able to create systems that develop and maintain this capability throughout the organizations they lead.

Digital transformation is one of the most significant trends shaping the future of business. As technology continues to advance, there is and will continue to be a growing need for team-wide approaches to utilize business intelligence software. The IQ, EQ, and PQ trio will play an essential role because it harnesses data and turns it into actionable insights.

The increasing and rapid adoption of artificial intelligence tools in enterprises will make the need for PQ even more acute. AI will help organizations harness data and simplify individual tasks. It will likely eliminate some individual contributor jobs. But the explosion of data inside the enterprise still needs to be captured, analyzed, harnessed, and *acted upon* for businesses to achieve their execution goals.

Additionally, the rise of remote work necessitates the development of more robust business acumen systems. Leaders must ensure that their teams, regardless of their physical locations, remain aligned with the organization's goals, and that they have access to the resources essential for effective collaboration and informed decision-making.

In this rapidly changing market environment, organizations must be adaptable. Rapid market changes require business processes that can respond swiftly to new challenges and opportunities. The synergy of IQ, EQ, and PQ can empower organizations to navigate these changes nimbly, thereby enabling them to swiftly capitalize on emerging opportunities while at the same time mitigating risks.

Moreover, in an era of heightened global competition, scalable business capabilities are indispensable. The seamless integration of IQ, EQ, and PQ enables organizations to devise strategies that can extend across borders and cultures so that it underpins expansive and sustainable growth. This comprehensive approach to business acumen will be vital in maintaining a competitive edge in the global market.

Conclusion

The Business Acumen Process represents a crucial application of Process Intelligence, transforming individual business acumen into organizational capability. By making strategic thinking and performance management simpler and more robust, organizations can create sustainable success that doesn't depend on individual leaders' capabilities.

This approach ensures that business acumen becomes embedded in organization's DNA rather than remaining locked in leaders' heads. The result is an organization that can maintain a high level of performance consistently, scale effectively, and develop future leaders systematically.

The key to success lies not in having the smartest leaders or the most sophisticated metrics, but rather, it lies in creating robust processes that make business intelligence accessible and actionable at all levels of the organization. As we'll explore in subsequent chapters, this systematic approach to business acumen forms the foundation for truly sustainable organizational excellence.

Workbook

Exercise 1: Metric Assessment - From Thermometer to Thermostat

Purpose

To evaluate your organization's current metrics and transform them from passive indicators to active drivers of business performance.

Steps

1. List your organization's top 10 metrics currently in use:

   1. _____

   2. _____

   [continue to 10]

2. For each metric, answer these diagnostic questions:

   - Is it clearly understood by everyone who uses it? (Y/N)

   - Can people directly influence this metric through their actions? (Y/N)

   - Does it drive specific actions when it's "red"? (Y/N)

   - Is there a clear owner accountable for this metric? (Y/N)

3. Transform Your Metrics:

   For any metric that received a "No," complete this action plan:
   ```

   Metric: _____

   Current State: _____

   To make this metric actionable, we need to:

   a) _____
   ```

b) _____

c) _____

Owner: _____

Timeline: _____

Exercise 2: Business Acumen Process Development

Purpose:

To create a systematic approach for developing and scaling business acumen throughout your organization.

Part A: Current State Assessment

Rate your organization's current state (1-5, where 1 is low and 5 is high):

```

```

___ Leaders can clearly explain how we make money

___ Employees understand how their work impacts business results

___ We have systematic processes for reviewing performance

___ Our metrics drive specific actions

___ We have clear corrective action protocols

___ Business acumen is consistently demonstrated across departments

Total Score: ___/30

Part B: Process Design

Based on your assessment, develop these key elements:

1. Education Process
```

How will we ensure people understand:
- Key business metrics: _____
- Value drivers: _____
- Business model: _____
2. Facilitation Process
Design your business review cadence:
Daily Huddles: _____
Weekly Reviews: _____
Monthly Business Reviews: _____
```

3. Iteration Process
```

How will we:
- Gather feedback: _____
- Adjust metrics: _____
- Improve processes: _____
```

Exercise 3: Are We Winning or Losing?

Purpose:
To develop a clear, systematic way to answer this fundamental question at any level of your organization.

 Part A: Define Victory
Complete this framework:

```
```

We are winning when:

1. _____

2. _____

3. _____

We are losing when:

1. _____

2. _____

3. _____
```
```

Part B: Create Your Process

Design your systematic approach:
```
```

1. Data Collection Process

   - What data do we need? _____

   - How often? _____

   2. Analysis Process

 - Who collects it? _____

   - Who analyzes? _____

   - What tools are needed? _____

   - How is it documented? _____

\3. Communication Process

   - Who needs to know? _____

   - How will we share it? _____

   - How often? _____

4. Action Process
   - Who decides on actions? _____
   - How are they tracked? _____
   - How do we ensure completion? ____

 Follow-up
Schedule a 90-day review to assess:
- How well is the process working?
- What adjustments are needed?
- Are we getting clearer answers to "Are we winning or losing?"

Reflection Questions

What was the most challenging part of these exercises?
What insights did you gain about your current metrics and processes?
What is your biggest opportunity for improvement?
What support do you need to implement these changes?
Remember: The goal is not perfection, but progress. Start with one area where you can make immediate improvements and build from there.

Chapter Six

Execution Process

From Feelings to Actions

A fundamental question reveals the true state of execution or the lack thereof in an organization:

"What have you done to move the business forward?"

Asking this simple question often reveals a gap between the knowledge someone possesses and whether it is being translated into actionable outcomes— demonstrating a huge gap between the creation of metrics and actually using them to make decisions and drive results. Many leaders, particularly those relying solely on the metrics of IQ and the interpersonal skills of EQ, inadvertently create cultures of dependency rather than instilling a sense of accountability among team members. These leaders frequently fall into the trap of stepping in to handle tasks that their teams could and should take care of themselves.

Why does this occur? Often, leaders who emphasize IQ and EQ rationalize this step-in-and-do-it approach as being quicker or more efficient, which underestimates the importance of empowering each team member to take ownership of his or her role and responsibilities. By overlooking and not instituting the practice of Process Intelligence in the execution phase, these leaders weaken their teams by establishing systems, perhaps inadvertently, that are entirely reliant on their continuous involvement.

In organizations lacking PQ, the reliance on leaders to constantly steer the ship can result in bottlenecks and prevent agile responses to new challenges from taking place. This not only inhibits growth. Teams miss opportunities to develop strategic thinking and execution skills. Without PQ, team members lack the framework and support needed to initiate and follow through on their initiatives independently.

This not only inhibits growth, but also the development of strategic thinking and execution skills. These organizations also ease cross-functional challenges. As a leader, how many times do you hear, "I wasn't able to get it done because I need something from another team"? We colloquially call that "sand in the gears." In high-functioning organizations, team members take actions and can raise the need for resources, usually time, money, or people, to solve problems.

By contrast, leaders who integrate PQ into the organization create environments in which accountability is ingrained and execution becomes a shared responsibility. They recognize that sustainable progress is achieved when teams are empowered to act decisively and confidently without the need for constant management intervention. This transformation from dependency to accountability not only enhances operational efficiency, it also cultivates a culture of continuous improvement and innovation, whereby every team member is able to actively contribute in ways that move the business forward.

The Execution Challenge: Emotion vs. Action

The Emotional Trap

In today's business environment, a significant challenge many organizations face is confusion surrounding the concepts of execution and accountability. As companies increasingly emphasize emotional intelligence, they often develop a skewed

The Challenge of Keeping Everyone's "HAPPY METER" on FULL!

One consequence of EQ "extreme thinking" is the belief that high functioning cultures are filled with happy people all the time. A place where engagement, ownership, and accountability are embraced collaboratively and easily. After 35 years, we at CSI can honestly say, this type of organization doesn't exist. However, it isn't for lack of trying by many leaders. Too often leaders have misaligned and misapplied the tenets of EQ creating organizations where they feel if I as the leader can just do for people, they will reciprocate in a manner that enables success. This is well intentioned and often shows up when the leader believes if they can just create a "happy" work environment, that employees will reciprocate with additional willingness, collaboration, and accountability. The leader mistakenly believes that in repetitive acts of benevolence, kindness, personal ownership, extreme empathy, that employees and teams will see such goodwill and in turn "feel" so positive about the organization that those "feelings" will translate into better results. Too often the only outcome is leadership fatigue as the leader is simply trying to keep everyone's "Happy Meter" FULL while theirs is running on fumes.

This isn't to say "Happiness" and "Feelings" aren't fundamental to a high functioning team, but rather, it is in the approach of getting there. PQ suggests that first and foremost a leader must connect people to what they have in common, not what they have in conflict. In the absence of shared purpose and commonalities, it is easy to devolve into grievance and unhappiness, forcing the leader to try as they might to charm, cajole, and convince those to believe in a different outcome. This simply further entrenches the organization in a non-sustainable personality driven operating model. High functioning leaders recognize that through common connectivity and the capacity to know if one is winning or losing is the only way to keep the proverbial "Happy Meter" on FULL!

understanding of what execution truly means, resulting in low-functioning behaviors that undermine organizational success.

By merging ideals such as ownership, involvement, empowerment, and engagement without a solid framework of processes, these organizations unintentionally dilute the essence of execution, transforming it from a concrete action into a more nebulous concept centered on emotion.

When execution is tethered primarily to emotions, it loses its clarity and precision. It becomes abstract and ambiguous, lacking a clear definition and direction. Execution driven by feeling can be temporal and fleeting, dependent on the mood, moment, and the current situation rather than on established goals and timelines.

This variable nature makes it highly dependent on individual interpretation, with each team member potentially seeing execution through a personal lens rather than through a unified standard. The result is a disconnection from measurable outcomes, where success is gauged subjectively in terms of emotions rather than by tangible and quantifiable results.

The Process Intelligence Solution

High-functioning organizations, however, take a different approach by applying the principles of Process Intelligence to define execution. In such organizations, execution is seen not as a mere feeling, but rather, as a concrete act—something that is demonstrative and objective. This redefinition focuses on actions that can be seen and measured, thus ensuring that every step taken by the organization has a clear, observable impact.

The key is moving from "how do I feel like we are doing" to "I know how we are doing, and more importantly, this is what I am doing to move the business forward."

When organizations systematically track and evaluate actions to ensure that they align with broader organizational goals, they improve individuals and teams' ability to get things done. This fosters a culture in which each action contributes to accomplishing strategic objectives and where outcomes are regularly assessed against metrics.

In other words, Process Intelligence enables organizations to create a culture of accountability and progress. They limit ambiguity and "feeling". This approach not only enhances operational efficiency, it also ensures that every team member is aligned with the organization's vision, contributing to sustainable and measurable success.

The improvements in employee engagement are demonstrable. Individuals can see where their contributions are tied to their team's success, and how their team contributes to the company's success. This linkage is truly powerful. The Gallup data citing incredibly low employee and manager engagement shows how necessary these changes are in most organizations. As we have shown in most of our case studies, organizations that embrace Process Intelligence see huge increases in employee engagement, along with other bottom line business metrics.

Low-Functioning vs High-Functioning Execution

In the landscape of organizational performance, execution is a critical differentiator between low-functioning and high-functioning organizations. The contrast between these two types of execution can often spell the difference between stagnation and sustained progress.

Low-Functioning Execution: Based on Feelings and Ambiguity

Leaders of organizations that operate with low-functioning execution often mistake the concept of execution for emotions. They intermingle ideas like ownership and empowerment with such inconsistency that accountability becomes a vague notion. In these environments, leaders are more concerned with how individuals feel about their tasks than they are about assessing what is actually being accomplished. This sentiment-driven approach results in accountability being abstract, ineffective, and lacking the substance needed to drive real business outcomes.

Moreover, such organizations frequently rely on *ignorance as an excuse.* They may permit teams to evade accountability by claiming a lack of awareness or information as a valid reason for inaction because, for example, "I didn't see that email," or "That's not my metric," or "I didn't know that was assigned to me." This fosters dependency on leadership for continuous guidance and reminders, further weakening individual responsibility and initiative.

Another hallmark of low-functioning execution is the idea that actions sent out after a meeting as "to dos" means they are an unimportant after thought, and even worse, the misuse of the action register, which is treated merely as another meeting device. Instead of serving as a tool to propel actions forward, it becomes just an artifact of meetings, existing alongside agendas and parking lots. This approach instills what we describe as a passive execution culture because it lacks urgency and the commitment to follow-through.

Additionally, these organizations host what can be termed as 'meeting tourists.' Participants attend meetings without making meaningful contributions because they merely observe rather than engage. This leads to meetings that, while informative, fail to catalyze the actionable change necessary for progress.

High-Functioning Execution: Focused on Demonstrative Actions and Accountability

Conversely, high-functioning organizations frame execution through the lens of demonstrative actions. They define execution with precision, through specific, measurable steps that are directly tied to moving the business forward. Leaders in these organizations prioritize concrete achievements and visible progress, ensuring that every action has a direct impact and positive impact on the metrics being measured every week, and therefore business results.

To eliminate the excuses rooted in ignorance, high-functioning organizations implement visible and measurable systems. Clear documentation and communication processes are established to ensure every action has an owner, a timeline, and a measurable outcome. These systems define responsibilities and deadlines, leaving no room for ambiguity or inaction.

In these environments, action registers transform into dynamic systems that not only track, but also drive results. Each action is linked to business metrics, accompanied by systematic follow-up processes that guarantee completion and assess effectiveness, thereby closing the loop on accountability.

Furthermore, high-functioning organizations cultivate *meeting drivers rather than meeting tourists.* Every attendee is expected and encouraged to actively participate, and to contribute specific, measurable actions that advance the organization's goals. This participatory culture ensures that meetings are not just platforms for information exchange, but rather, that they are instrumental in driving forward actionable plans.

By transitioning from a culture rooted in feelings to one of demonstrative action and comprehensive accountability, leaders of organizations can create an environment in which members consistently move the business toward the accomplishment of objectives.

The PQ Execution Process

1. Data-Action Alignment

In the landscape of high-functioning execution, a critical element supporting this is the alignment of data and action. This involves tying metrics directly to corrective actions to ensure that insights lead directly to improved results.

Business Acumen: Understanding Our Position

At the heart of this alignment is the concept of business acumen, which as stated earlier centers on the fundamental question: "Are we winning or losing?" High-functioning organizations constantly assess their performance against goals and benchmarks, gaining a clear understanding of their competitive position and operational effectiveness. Even lower level employees understand what winning is to them. They measure output, on time, units, quality, safety and so forth. This insight provides the necessary context for informed decision-making, ensuring that everyone in the organization is aware of where they stand.

Connecting the "Shop Floor to the Top Floor"

Operational effectiveness is nothing if not visible. An organization's communication cadence is the system to "Bring Visibility to Accountability." This operational effectiveness is best seen through the cadence of Organizational Tier Meetings.

Tier Five – CEO and Division Leaders
Tier Four – Division Leaders and Site Leaders
Tier Three – Site Leader and Departmental Managers
Tier Two – Departmental Managers and Supervisors
Tier One – Supervisors and Employees

Each of these Tier Meetings should be sequenced to launch at the beginning of the week driven by the team's business acumen process. Did we win the previous week? If we did, let's affirm and recognize, and if we lost, let's drive corrective actions.

This PQ mindset of Operational Effectiveness is driven weekly through each Tier with the lowest Tier (Tier One) having an Area Information Center (AIC Board) where the Tier will gather to discuss common operational effectiveness questions:

1. Safety – Did everyone go home the same way they arrived?
2. Quality – Did the products/services we delivered today meet and exceed our quality standards? Did anything we produced today get put on hold or get sent back?
3. Delivery – Did we meet our production/volume goal today? Did we execute what we promised to our internal or external customers?
4. People – Did we have proper staffing? Did everyone come in today? Do we need to plan for any vacations or upcoming training sessions?
5. Cost – Did we have any unplanned waste today?

This type of metric driven Tier One AIC Meeting is a cornerstone of high functioning organizations and is at the heart of understanding operational effectiveness.

Ironically, many CSI clients are swimming in data, metrics, and dashboards before we begin working with them. The key in high-functioning organizations is to boil all that down to a few key metrics, *only those you need, the ones that drive the business forward.*

Action Implementation: Moving from Insight to Action

Equally important is the need to translate this knowledge into action. As has been said, whether this is the case can be illuminated by the answer to the question:

"What are we going to do about it?"

High-functioning execution demands that teams and individuals not only understand their current business situation but also take decisive steps that address challenges and leverage opportunities. This involves concrete actions, with owners, and dates, that are directly tied to the insights gained from business acumen.

Together, the alignment of business acumen and action implementation ensures that an organization's members are not only aware of their performance but are also actively engaged in processes that drive improvement and success. This dynamic connection between understanding and doing is what propels organizations forward to achieve their objectives.

2. The Action Register System

The cornerstone of high-functioning execution in any organization is the Action Register System, a carefully crafted approach to action management that aligns every step with strategic business objectives. It starts with action documentation, where each task is outlined with a clear description. This ensures that everyone involved understands exactly what needs to be done and how it fits into the bigger picture.

Every action documented in the system is directly linked to business metrics, reinforcing the connection between task completion and organizational success. By doing so, actions are not isolated activities but integral parts of a larger strategy. To maintain clarity and accountability, specific ownership is assigned to every task. This ensures that there is an individual responsible for driving the action all the way to completion, eliminating any ambiguity regarding responsibility.

Moreover, defined completion criteria are established, providing a clear standard for determining when an action has been successfully executed. This clarity helps to maintain focus and in measuring effectiveness.

The Action Register System also incorporates a systematic review process. Regular status updates are essential components of this process, which act as checkpoints to track progress and identify areas that may require adjustments. These updates feed into performance tracking—a continuous activity that ensures actions are contributing effectively towards strategic objectives.

Accountability enforcement is another important aspect. By holding each action owner accountable, the system ensures commitments are met and follow-through is guaranteed. Finally, result verification is conducted to confirm that actions have yielded the desired outcomes. This step not only validates success but also supplies a feedback loop for ongoing improvement.

Through the Action Register System, organizations can achieve a harmonious blend of planning and practice, thereby ensuring that every action taken is purposeful, accountable, and directly supportive of their business goals.

This may sound like an onerous management style. In fact, our clients really embrace it. Having all team members accountable for their actions highlights the positive momentum that individuals, teams, and companies are making toward their goals. It drives significant improvements in employee engagement. People *like* knowing how their work contributes to the enterprise's success.

3. The Six Tenets of High-Functioning Execution

The Six Tenets of High-Functioning Execution bridge together organizational successes by ensuring that every action is part of a cohesive, strategic effort. At the heart of these tenets is **Systematic Integration**, where action registers are employed in every meeting to ensure issues are addressed and tracked consistently. This "bolt-on" strategy targets underperforming metrics directly, focusing efforts where they are most needed, while maintaining a clear connection to the overall business scorecard.

Closely linked to this is **Metric-Action Alignment**. In high-functioning organizations, every metric that is falling short—each of which is indicated in red—necessitates a documented corrective action. This demands a direct connection between metrics and the actions taken to address them, ensuring clear ownership and accountability are in place to drive results.

Clarity and Specificity are paramount in High Functioning execution. Too often, teams have attempted to adopt the meeting tool of an Action Log, Action Register, or Action Item list. Organizations often learned this tool was essential when they provided leaders with training on how to run an effective meeting. The Action Register was discussed in the same vein as an agenda, parking lot, meeting ground rule, etc. When the team went to use the Action Register they attempted to capture actions when they heard words like, "Who is going to take action? Someone should, can you, I will..." These are action statements, but without the context of connectivity they are often lost, ignored, or captured in such a cryptic way, they only serve to create ambiguity and frustration because no one truly remembers the interpretation, purpose or meaning at the next meeting. Often the action register is abandoned due to lack of clarity and specificity.

At CSI, we believe a robust Action Register is the mechanism that make metrics "thermostatic," bolting on to underperforming metrics a clear and connected action is a high functioning behavior of great teams. Creating a narrative of performance and corrective actions allows the team to demonstrate business acumen and effective execution. At CSI we promote the creation of actions written with "12 month clarity" meaning, a member of the team could pick an action register up a day, week, month, or year later and the action would be written with such a degree of clarity and specificity that they would still remember the purpose, scope, and intent of the action. This is a fundamental process in high functioning organizations. Without it, ignorance as an excuse is tough to overcome.

Detailed documentation removes ambiguity, while clear success criteria guide efforts towards concrete outcomes, ensuring everyone understands what success looks like and how it will be measured.

The tenet of **Formal Ownership** emphasizes explicit action acceptance, eliminating the possibility of "drive-by" assignments where responsibilities are unclear. By defining clear responsibility channels, organizations instill accountability and ensure tasks are completed by the right people.

Intentional Timing focuses on the thoughtful setting of due dates, factoring in available resources and aligning priorities. This ensures actions are feasible and appropriately synchronized with other organizational activities, optimizing resource allocation and strategic focus.

Finally, the **Renegotiation Protocol** provides a clear process for making adjustments to timelines. By requiring advance notification and taking a systematic approach to any changes, this tenet ensures that all parties are informed and prepared to adapt without disrupting overall execution.

Breaking the Dependency Cycle

The Personal Action Register

To transform team members from dependent followers into accountable and proactive performers, the Personal Action Register offers a structured approach to individual accountability and development. At its core, this system begins with thorough **Documentation**.

Each action item includes clear requirements, ensuring that team members understand exactly what needs to be achieved. Specific responsibility assignments are made, delineating who is accountable for each task, while defined timelines keep projects on track and provide measurable goals. Regular follow-up protocols establish a routine of checking progress and maintaining momentum toward completion.

Complementing these elements is a dedicated **Coaching Process**, designed to support skill development and empower team members to perform at their best. Through progress monitoring, the effectiveness of these development initiatives is evaluated, ensuring that team members are advancing as expected.

Accountability enforcement is woven into the process, instilling a sense of ownership and drive to meet objectives. Throughout this journey, performance feedback plays a critical role, offering constructive insights that help individuals refine their skills and grow in their roles.

By instilling these practices, the Personal Action Register not only breaks the cycle of dependency but also cultivates a culture of responsibility and performance within the team.

Case Study: Breaking the Dependency Cycle at REVLON

A Journey from Conceptual Involvement to Real Accountability

When REVLON embarked on the implementation of the Process Based Leadership® Personal Action Register system, it was amid a pressing operational challenge. At the time, leaders were solving 70% of issues presented by their teams, which led to an average daily expenditure of 2.5 hours on routine tasks. Despite comprehensive training initiatives aimed at fostering empowerment, the organization continued to experience a

REVLON®

Date:_____

PERSONAL ACTION REGISTER

Action	R	T	C

"Our People are the source for providing innovative, high quality, and cost competitive beauty products."

Legend: **R** - Responsible, **T** - Target Date, **C** - Completion Date

Provided by CSI - 1-800-246-8694

A leader fills out this form with the name of the one to take action & gives it to that person, who then is obligated to follow through.

substantial reliance on supervisors for problem-solving, underscoring a disconnect in their efforts to embed accountability within their culture.

The core problem was a high dependency on supervisors, who were routinely tasked with resolving issues that could be managed by the associates themselves. This was compounded by a significant disconnect between accountability concepts taught in training sessions and the practices implemented in daily operations. Limited employee initiative and engagement resulted from inconsistency in their approach to resolving problems.

To address these challenges, REVLON implemented a series of strategic interventions centered around the Personal Action Register system. Leaders began consistently using Personal

Action Registers, which served as a tangible tool for promoting accountability. They also established systematic protocols to ensure that issues were tracked and resolved in a timely and efficient manner.

Working with CSI, the business significantly changed their structure of meetings, introducing clear documentation requirements for actions, including outcomes, and responsibilities. Regular accountability reviews were also put into place that improved communication between leaders and associates about expectations, progress, and areas for improvement.

The results were transformative. Team members developed a sharper judgment about which issues genuinely required leadership intervention, and this led to a significant reduction in trivial complaints. The shift in perspective also empowered employees to engage in more self-directed problem-solving, reducing unnecessary escalation of issues to supervisors.

Over time, the organization evolved from one of dependency to one that exhibited an interdependency of leader-associate relationships. Leaders and associates began to collaborate more effectively, sharing responsibility for outcomes that created a work environment characterized by mutual respect and shared accountability.

The introduction of the Personal Action Register profoundly revolutionized how team members and leaders worked. Post-implementation, the organization experienced an 85% reduction in the time leaders dedicated to problem-solving. Rather than remaining mired in daily operational issues, this shift enabled them to redirect their focus towards strategic tasks and mentoring. Concurrently, team members exhibited a remarkable 60% increase in engagement. They started to tackle problems more proactively, significantly enhancing their engagement and personal development within the company.

Moreover, the company saw a 40% improvement in the speed of issue resolution. This enhancement can be attributed to team members taking a more active role in addressing challenges, facilitated by the clear documentation and accountability procedures introduced by the Personal Action Register. Additionally, these changes led to a significant decrease in leader stress levels, as they no longer bore the weight of daily problem-solving alone.

The critical insight gained from this transformation was that it extended beyond merely saving time or reducing workload. The initiative fundamentally reshaped the organization's approach to problem-solving and accountability.

By fostering an environment where responsibility was shared and solutions were sourced collaboratively, REVLON cultivated a robust culture of empowerment and efficiency. This case underscores the profound impact that structured accountability systems can have on operational dynamics, and it illuminates the potential for widespread change when teams are both equipped and entrusted to drive results.

The 90-Day Accountability Analysis

To ensure sustained high performance, implement regular accountability analyses:

Analysis Components

This process is designed to keep a pulse on how tasks and initiatives are being carried out and whether they lead to consistent, long-term success. The analysis comprises various components, each offering unique insights into the organization's operations and performance.

At the heart of this analysis is Action Tracking, which monitors the number of actions taken and their completion rates. By keeping track of how many tasks are executed and how efficiently they are completed, leaders and members of organizations can gauge operational effectiveness. Beyond just counting tasks, this component also involves a value assessment to enable them to understand the impact and significance of each action within the broader organizational context.

Equally significant is Engagement Measurement, which focuses on evaluating participation levels across the team. This involves observing who is actively participating, who is demonstrating initiative, and assessing the overall impact of each individual's contributions. By measuring engagement, organizations can discern the depth of involvement from each team member and identify contributors who are leading new initiatives or significantly enhancing team dynamics.

Lastly, Performance Evaluation enables a comprehensive look at individual and team performance. This component involves assessing individual contributions, reviewing team effectiveness, and analyzing system efficiency. By evaluating these aspects, leaders of organizations can determine how well individuals and teams are performing in relation to established objectives, identify areas for potential improvement, and get ready for implementation.

Implementation Steps

A structured approach to implementation is essential in order to bring the 90-Day Accountability Analysis to life. This process spans several key steps, starting with meticulous data collection. This begins by gathering comprehensive data from action registers and includes detailing the completion rates of actions. Moreover, it is important to assess the value of each action in order to understand its significance within the organization's broader objectives. This data sets the foundation for subsequent analysis.

With the data in hand, the next phase involves conducting a thorough analysis. During this step, engagement patterns are identified and team members evaluated with respect to their participation and contribution to the various initiatives undertaken. This involves closely examining individual contributions in order to measure the level of engagement and commitment exhibited by each. In addition, assessing team dynamics typically provides insights concerning how well teams are collaborating with one another. Not surprisingly, such an analysis will typically expose issues and areas requiring enhancement or intervention.

Finally, the process culminates with Action Planning where insights from the analysis are translated into strategies for improvement. This involves developing actionable plans intended to enhance performance, making necessary adjustments to existing systems, and implementing corrective measures wherever they are needed. By doing so, any gaps or inefficiencies can be addressed to ensure that things are continuously moving towards improved accountability and performance. This approach ensures that the accountability analysis not only provides a snapshot of current performance, but that it also actively informs future strategy and operations.

Creating Sustainable Execution

From Meeting Tourists to Meeting Drivers

Making consistent and sustainable execution happen within an organization requires a transformational approach, especially when addressing the issue of "meeting tourism." In low-functioning organizations, meetings often become unproductive gatherings where those in attendance do not actively contribute with the result that there is minimal if any impact on the business. In contrast, high-functioning organizations foster "meeting drivers" by implementing strategic initiatives designed to engage and energize participants.

First and foremost, it is crucial to establish clear expectations. This involves defining and setting participation requirements for all attendees, thus ensuring that each individual understands his or her role and what is expected of them. Specific contribution metrics are introduced that produce tangible measures of how effectively each participant contributes to discussions and decision-making. Additionally, regular performance evaluations help reinforce these expectations and serve to create a culture in which everyone is held accountable for their participation and impact.

The institution of systematic accountability further enables this transformation. High-functioning organizations conduct 90-day engagement assessments to track and analyze participation levels over time. This ongoing evaluation produces clear contribution metrics, enabling leaders to identify areas where improvement is needed. A robust feedback mechanism also provides participants with actionable insights into their engagement and highlighting opportunities for growth and improvement.

Finally, a focus on development ensures that participants are equipped with the necessary skills to contribute meaningfully. This includes offering skill-building opportunities to enhance competencies, leadership development programs to cultivate emerging leaders, and performance coaching to address individual growth areas.

By committing to continuous development, organizations empower their teams to move from passive participants to active contributors who drive meeting outcomes and organizational success.

Through these efforts, organizations can transition from low-functioning environments plagued by passive attendance to high-performing cultures where sustainable execution is the norm and every meeting serves as a catalyst for progress.

Over the past 20 years leading diverse teams, I've found few frameworks as impactful as Process Based Leadership®—the system developed by my friend and longtime colleague, Shane Yount and the amazing team at Competitive Solutions. Their work has not only guided me as a leader but has empowered the teams I've served to build cultures rooted in accountability, clarity, and continuous improvement. Their insights offer both new and seasoned leaders a practical, proven path to drive productivity and foster ownership at every level. Having worked alongside Shane and the CSI team through the years, I've seen firsthand the power of their approach, and I continue to be inspired by their leadership. I only wish I had discovered their work earlier in my career—it would have made a world of difference.

Matt Pearson,
Vice President, Quality System & Risk Management

⬤ GUARDANT

Conclusion

The shift from emotion-based analysis to action-based execution is a key step in the effort to improve organizational effectiveness when it comes to the procedures to be used to achieve business goals. By embracing Process Intelligence in execution, leaders can establish sustainable systems that cultivate independence and resilience. In doing so, they move beyond the limitations of teams that rely excessively on their guidance. Rather than sporadic results that hinge on inconsistent efforts, organizations realize consistent and reliable outcomes that drive long-term success.

Through this approach, teams embrace collective accountability, which fosters an environment in which every member shares responsibility for success—instead of only a select few. By moving away from subjective assessments to rely upon clear evidence of progress, execution transforms into a measurable, objective process. Such clarity allows organizations to track and refine performance continuously, thereby ensuring close alignment with strategic goals.

The core of Process Intelligence execution is not about leaders doing more for their teams. It is about crafting systems that empower individuals to achieve greater successes independently. This transformation of business understanding into concrete action is facilitated through systematic, sustainable processes that clearly focus on execution.

Ultimately, it's important to keep in mind that execution is not governed by feelings or personal preferences. It is an expectation that manifests through clear, visible actions that tangibly move the business forward. By adopting this mindset and leveraging Process Intelligence, organizations can effectively and sustainably achieve their stated objectives.

Workbook

Exercise 1: From Feelings to Actions

Purpose:

Transform emotional or abstract commitments into concrete, measurable actions.

Steps

1. List your top 3 current team or departmental goals:

   1. _____

   2. _____

   3. _____

2. For each goal, complete:

Goal: _____

Current Status: Red or Green? _____

If Red:

Specific Action Required: _____

Who Owns It: _____

Due Date: _____

How Will We Measure Success? _____

Exercise 2: Action Register Audit

Purpose:

Evaluate your current action tracking system and transform it from a meeting device to an accountability system.

Steps

1. Review your last month of actions:

Total Actions: _____
Actions Completed On Time: _____
Actions Still Open: _____
Actions Without Clear Owner: _____

2. Answer these diagnostic questions:
   - Does each action have a clear "moved the business forward" outcome? Y/N
   - Is each action linked to a specific business metric? Y/N
   - Do we follow up on actions between meetings? Y/N
   - Do we have a clear process for renegotiating due dates? Y/N

3. Create your new action tracking process:

How will we:
   - Document new actions: _____
   - Follow up between meetings: _____
   - Handle missed deadlines: _____
   - Celebrate completions: _____

Exercise 3: Meeting Performance Assessment

Purpose:

Transform meeting participants from tourists to drivers.

Steps

1. Score your last three meetings (1-5 scale):
   ```

   Meeting Date: _____

   - Clear actions created: _____
   - Actions had owners & dates: _____
   - All participants contributed: _____
   - Previous actions reviewed: _____

   Total Score: _____/20

2. Plan your next meeting:

   Before Meeting:
   - Pre-work required: _____
   - Actions to be reviewed: _____

   During Meeting:
   - How will we ensure participation: _____
   - How will we document new actions: _____

   After Meeting:
   - How will we follow up: _____
   - When will we check progress: _____
   Remember:
   - Focus on actions, not intentions
   - Make everything visible and measurable
   - Create systems, not one-time fixes
   - Drive accountability through clarity
   ```

Chapter Seven
Communication Process
From Information to Action

In our journey through Process Intelligence leadership, we've explored how Business Acumen provides the framework for understanding the key question, "Are we winning or losing?" and how the Execution Process transforms that knowledge into action through the question, "What have you done to move the business forward?" Now we have arrived at the third critical system: the Communication Process, where these elements converge in the fundamental question:

"Did the time we just spent move our business forward?"

The modern workplace often drowns in information, yet it thirsts for meaningful communication. Consider a typical day in most organizations: Leaders sprint from meeting to meeting, their calendars are packed from dawn to dusk. Team members wade through hundreds of emails, their inboxes overflowing with updates, requests, and FYIs. Bulletin boards display metrics that few stop to read, while chat notifications constantly demand attention. Companies invest in sophisticated communication platforms, virtual meeting tools, and collaboration software, and yet the fundamental question remains: "Is any of this actually moving the business forward?"

The cost of this communication chaos is staggering. Studies show that executives spend up to 80% of their time in meetings, leaving precious little space for strategic thinking or actual execution. Team members report feeling simultaneously overwhelmed by information yet uninformed about what really matters. The rise of remote work has only intensified these challenges, with virtual meetings multiplying and screen fatigue becoming a universal complaint. Meanwhile, critical business information often fails to reach those who need it most, or it arrives too late to drive meaningful action.

This communication crisis reveals a fundamental truth: more information doesn't equal better communication. Organizations have mastered the art of information sharing, but they struggle with the science of driving action through effective communication. They excel at broadcasting messages, but they falter at creating the two-way engagement that moves businesses forward. What is the result? A workplace full of noise but starved for clarity—one rich in data, but poor in understanding—one abundant in meetings, but lacking momentum.

The solution lies not in adding more communication tools, or in training better communicators. It lies in creating systematic processes that transform communication from an activity into a driver of business results. This is where Process Intelligence (PQ) can make a critical difference. It can do so by building upon the foundations of Business Acumen and Execution to create a communication system that consistently delivers results.

The Integration Challenge

The previous chapters laid two crucial foundations. The Business Acumen Process laid out a fundamental of organizational performance by creating clear metrics and scorecards that tell us if we're winning or losing. The Execution Process transformed this knowledge into action by moving us from feeling-based to action-based accountability.

The challenge of the Communication Process is to integrate these systems in such a way that drives organizational performance. This integration must overcome common barriers: meeting overload, information silos, and the perennial gap between knowing and doing.

Overcoming Communication Barriers

Organizations typically face three major communication challenges that Process Intelligence must address:

Time Consumption

Traditional communication approaches often waste valuable time through unfocused meetings, redundant messages, and inefficient information flow. Process Intelligence communication reclaims this time by creating structured, purposeful interactions that directly drive business results.

Information Overload

Many organizations mistake more information for better communication, overwhelming teams with data while failing to drive action. Process Intelligence cuts through this noise by focusing communication on *metrics that matter* and actions that move the business forward.

Accountability Gaps

Without systematic communication processes, accountability becomes personality-dependent and inconsistent. Process Intelligence closes these gaps by creating clear connections between metrics, actions, and results.

Low vs. High-Functioning Communication

In a low-functioning communication environment, the process resembles advertising—a largely one-way street. Reliance on bulletin boards, email broadcasts, and newsletters fosters a culture of passive engagement. This lack of dynamic interaction provides an easy scapegoat for anyone and everyone. Ignorance becomes an excuse for missing out on critical information. Meetings in such organizations are viewed as mere additions to the workweek, seen as interruptions rather than necessary gatherings that enhance productivity. With their calendars bloated by endless, unproductive sessions, leaders perceive them as distractions from the "real work."

Employees in these settings often find themselves lost in a swamp of meetings, spending 60% to 80% of their work week in sessions that rarely provide value. Cameras remain off, and engagement is minimal as meetings become tick-box exercises rather than opportunities for collaboration and decision-making.

The purpose of such meetings is frequently muddled, leading to dissatisfaction aired in hallways rather than improvements generated within the walls of the meeting room. Leadership's presence is a crutch, with meetings often scrapped if the leader can't attend, thus highlighting a dependency on personality over process.

Conversely, in a high-functioning communication environment, the focus shifts to communicating in two-way, face-to-face dialogues that ensure accountability and dispel ignorance. Important topics are intently discussed in an environment in which information flows freely and decision-making is informed. Such meetings are seen as enablers—crucial business drivers that help set the company's tempo, focus, and future actions.

Each session is designed to propel the business forward. Reinforced by clear metrics and actionable objectives, meetings maintain a clear business focus, and leaders consistently ask whether they've succeeded in advancing company goals through systematic review and ongoing improvement.

These meetings operate with a non-negotiable cadence, transcending reliance on any one individual. They are so ingrained in the organization's rhythm that they continue seamlessly regardless of a leader's presence, underscoring a commitment to process and structure over dependency on personality.

Thus, moving from a low-functioning to a high-functioning communication model involves embracing a collaborative, process-driven mentality that ensures every dialogue and decision meaningfully contributes to organizational success.

Integrating IQ, EQ, and PQ in Communication

Effective communication requires the integration of all three intelligence dimensions:

The IQ Component

Incorporating Intelligence Quotient into communication practices requires a strategic approach that transcends the mere exchange of information. Unfortunately, many organizations fall into the trap of equating intelligence with an overload of information, inundating teams with mountains of data devoid of context or clarity.

Leaders need to adopt a focused approach by identifying critical business metrics that merit monitoring in order to truly harness IQ in organizational communication. This begins with the ability to identify critical business metrics that merit a team's attention. One of the keys here is to determine which projects, metrics, and goals have a direct impact on achieving strategic objectives, and then placing the emphasis on these in communications.

Moreover, effective leaders analyze trends and patterns that affect business performance by extracting valuable insights from raw data. Adopting such an analytical lens allows them to foresee potential challenges and opportunities within a market landscape.

Communication should also include the ability to translate complex data into actionable insights. This requires distilling vast amounts of information into digestible formats that guide decision-making and direct clear actions. By doing so, leaders ensure that their teams are equipped with the knowledge necessary to act decisively and purposefully.

Lastly, structuring communication around key business drivers ensures alignment across the organization. Each message should tie back to core objectives, thereby reinforcing the path forward and ensuring that everyone is consistently moving in the right direction.

Through these strategies, communication becomes not just an exchange of information but a catalyst for strategic action and organizational success.

The EQ Component

Emotional Intelligence is a vital element for leaders aiming to genuinely understand and connect with their teams. However, it should not function in isolation. When organizations depend excessively on charismatic leaders to maintain engagement, rather than establishing sustainable communication systems, they risk developing a debilitating reliance on personalities.

EQ empowers leaders in several key ways that enhance organizational communication. It allows them to read team dynamics during meetings, recognizing unspoken cues and emotions that can influence the flow and outcome of discussions. This understanding is crucial for managing group interactions effectively and to ensure every voice is heard and valued.

Additionally, EQ encourages leaders to adjust their communication style for different audiences. Recognizing that individuals have unique ways of processing information and emotions, adaptable leaders can tailor their approach so that it resonates more deeply with diverse team members, enhancing clarity and receptivity.

Building trust through authentic dialogue is another significant advantage of EQ. When leaders engage in open, sincere conversations, they create a foundation of trust that encourages team members to share their thoughts and ideas more freely. This trust is integral to fostering a collaborative and innovative work environment.

Moreover, EQ aids leaders in navigating difficult

conversations effectively. By managing their own emotions and empathizing with others, they can address challenging issues with tact and sensitivity, ensuring that even the toughest discussions lead to constructive outcomes.

By weaving these EQ capabilities into their communication practices, leaders facilitate not only personal connections but also a cohesive and robust organizational culture that is less reliant on individual personalities and more dependent on holistic, sustainable communication systems.

The PQ Component

Process Intelligence shifts the paradigm of communication from one driven by individual personalities to that of a systematic and strategic business function. It introduces a disciplined approach that ensures consistent and effective communication throughout the organization.

The key elements of a PQ-driven communication strategy include a structured meeting agenda focused on business metrics. This ensures that discussions are centered around crucial metrics that directly impact the organization's strategic objectives so that every interaction has a clear purpose and direction.

Another critical element is the integration of scorecard reviews and action registers into the communication process. This involves regularly assessing business performance through dynamic scorecards, discussing outcomes, and maintaining a clear action register. This register tracks responsibilities and timelines to ensure that actions are followed through efficiently.

Implementing clear protocols for follow-up and accountability is essential. After discussions, established protocols ensure that follow-ups are conducted systematically and that they promote accountability and drive results. This structure minimizes ambiguity and maximizes productivity by making it clear who is responsible for each task and when each one should be completed.

A systematic approach to meeting effectiveness ensures that every meeting is productive. By setting clear objectives, preparing participants, allocating time wisely, and reviewing outcomes with the objective of improving future meetings, leaders can improve meeting productively.

By embedding these disciplined PQ methodologies into communication processes, leaders of organizations enhance clarity, consistency, and efficiency and thereby turning communication into a robust driver of business performance.

The Six-Hour Meeting Week

In the quest for improved efficiency and streamlined communication, high-functioning organizations have adopted a disciplined six-hour meeting framework that aligns their operational and strategic efforts. This structured approach encapsulates three distinct yet interrelated segments: Strategic Review, Operational Review, and Team Development. Each segment is meticulously designed to address key facets of organizational performance, ensuring both clarity and productivity.

Strategic Review (2 hours)

The Strategic Review segment focuses on aligning the organization's long-term objectives with current performance metrics. It begins with a comprehensive scorecard review where leadership assesses key metrics to ensure that the organization's

Only Six Hours of Meetings a Week?

"How many meetings does it take to run a high functioning team? How many hours a week should a leader be in meetings?" These are common questions we receive at CSI. Our answer may surprise you – Our data suggests that leaders should be able to run their businesses in six hours of meetings a week or less.

HOW?? Through communication systems that allow leaders to operate from a position of offense. What does a position of offense look like? It's when Thermostatic Metrics drive the meeting. It's when those metrics are used to drive corrective action, demonstrate a sense of urgency, and affirm positive momentum.

In the absence of Thermostatic Metrics as the meeting driver and purpose, leaders find themselves in a "Doom Loop" where content is redundant, participation is marginal, and overall frustration is high. Breaking the "Meeting Doom Loop" requires a wholesale meeting review – At CSI, we refer to this as "Deconstruct to Reconstruct" – A deconstruction of the current meeting cadence with an analytical lens on functionality, quality, and content.

Too often meetings are launched and never reviewed for effectiveness. When applying a PQ lens, CSI has found we can eliminate 30% of initial meetings and restructure the remaining 70% with a system driven process that gives the highest probability that the meeting will actually, "Move the business forward!"

trajectory remains aligned with its strategic vision. This is followed by strategic action planning, which is a collaborative effort to devise actionable plans that address gaps and capitalize on opportunities identified during the scorecard evaluation.

Crucial to this segment is cross-functional coordination, where departments synchronize efforts in order to foster an environment of unified purpose across the organization. Finally, resource allocation decisions are made, thereby allocating necessary resources to ensure strategic initiatives can be effectively executed without unnecessary delays.

Operational Review (2 hours)

The Operational Review segment allows teams to delve into daily performance metrics to create a snapshot of the organization's real-time health. By focusing on immediate performance and operational efficiency, it emphasizes immediate issue resolution and empowers teams to quickly address and mitigate operational challenges.

By updating the action register, the organization ensures that tasks are tracked and accountability is clear, paving the way for consistent follow-through. Furthermore, team coordination is reinforced by enabling teams to adjust workflows and priorities as necessary to maintain optimal performance.

Team Development (2 hours)

The final segment, Team Development, emphasizes the growth and cohesion of the workforce. It begins with sessions for skills and knowledge sharing, allowing team members to learn from one another and to stay abreast of best practices. This is complemented by discussions on process improvement, where they work together to seek out efficiencies and innovations in their workflows.

Recognizing and celebrating achievements is crucial, which is why this segment includes recognition and celebration to motivate and acknowledge contributions. Lastly, it focuses on team building and alignment to foster a collaborative culture and ensure that team efforts remain in sync with organizational goals.

Creating a Process Intelligence Communication System

The key to effective communication lies in creating a system that integrates Business Acumen and Execution through structured processes:

Standard Meeting Agenda

Every effective meeting follows a clear structure that drives business results:

Action Register Review (15%): This initial segment focuses on accountability and progress assessment. Teams review previous actions, ensuring that each task's completion status is updated. Any barriers to completion are addressed, allowing teams to strategize about overcoming challenges and ensuring consistent follow-through.

Scorecard Review (30%): A significant portion of the meeting is dedicated to evaluating performance metrics. Teams conduct a review of current metrics and identify areas that need improvement. Special emphasis is placed on creating action plans for red metrics, which are indicators of deviation from expected performance, to ensure that corrective measures are prioritized.

Team Input and Discussion (20%): Open dialogue is encouraged during this segment, allowing team members to share operational updates and to address emerging issues. This collaborative approach ensures that coordinated activities are streamlined so that a unified effort is maintained across the team.

Recognition (10%): Celebrating successes is important to

maintain high morale. This agenda item focuses on celebrating successes and acknowledging the contributions of team members. Sharing best practices not only highlights achievements but also promotes a culture of learning and continuous improvement.

Information Flow (15%): Effective communication hinges on the clear dissemination of information. The meeting includes time to share critical updates and to cascade key messages to ensure and maintain alignment across all levels of the organization. Gathering feedback during this time allows leadership to stay attuned to team concerns and suggestions.

Action Confirmation (5%): As the meeting concludes, reviewing and confirming new actions is crucial. Teams ensure ownership and deadlines are clearly defined so that clarity exists concerning next steps required to maintain momentum and ensure accountability.

Meeting Effectiveness Audit (5%): A brief evaluation of the meeting's success rounds out the agenda. Teams evaluate meeting effectiveness and identify areas for improvement that will enhance future meetings. Planning adjustments for the next meeting ensures that the meeting process remains dynamic and responsive to organizational needs.

Meeting Effectiveness Protocol

The question must be asked and an answer given for every meeting: "Did this move the business forward?" This requires systematic evaluation through four key lenses:

Metric Impact

Meetings must establish a direct connection to business metrics to ensure that discussions and outcomes are aligned with the organization's key performance indicators. Evaluating clear movement toward goals is imperative because a meeting should deliver actionable insights that drive progress. To assess this effectively, the presence of measurable progress indicators is crucial because this enables teams to gauge the meeting's impact on strategic objectives, quantitatively.

Action Clarity

Every meeting should conclude with specific, assigned actions, leaving no ambiguity about what needs to be done next. Clear ownership and deadlines for each action ensure accountability because team members understand their responsibilities as well as the timeframes for them to be accomplished. A systematic follow-up process is vital because it allows teams to track the execution of these actions and it provides a foundation for evaluating future progress.

Engagement Quality

Collective efforts serve to enhance a meeting's output, which is why we maintain that high-quality engagement is characterized by active participation by all attendees, particularly when each person's input is valued and utilized. All attendees should make meaningful contributions, thereby reinforcing a collaborative and inclusive approach to problem solving and continuous improvement efforts.

Time Effectiveness

Efficient meeting management requires the effective use of meeting time. This is facilitated through the use of a structured meeting agenda that prioritizes the most critical discussions. By focusing on priority items, attention is directed to issues that most directly influence the ability to accomplish strategic goals. Elimination of non-value activities helps prevent time wastage, while maintaining a sharp focus on delivering results is what is most likely to drive the business forward.

Conclusion

The Communication Process represents the culmination of Process Intelligence Leadership, where Business Acumen and Execution come together in systematic, effective dialogue. Success requires moving beyond both information sharing and emotional connection to create robust processes that drive business results.

The journey from low-functioning to high-functioning communication isn't about better tools or more charismatic leaders. It's about creating systematic processes that make communication a genuine business driver. When organizations achieve this transformation, they reclaim productive time, drive consistent action, and create sustainable success.

By integrating Business Acumen and Execution processes into a systematic communication cadence, organizations create a powerful engine for sustainable performance improvement. This integration ensures that every conversation, every meeting, and every interaction moves the business forward in meaningful, measurable ways.

Chapter Eight
Ideal Behavior Process
From Expectations to Excellence

In our journey through Process Intelligence Leadership, we've established three pivotal systems: Business Acumen, which answers the essential question, "Are we winning or losing?" The Execution Process, which addresses "What have you done to move the business forward?" And the Communication Process, designed to ensure that our collective time is dedicated to driving tangible results. As we delve deeper into this framework, we now encounter perhaps the most fundamental inquiry:

"Are we living up to, or are we falling short of our ideal behaviors?"

This question strikes at the core of organizational effectiveness and sustainability. While metrics indicate our competitive standing, actions highlight our progress, and communication fosters alignment, it is our behaviors that ultimately determine whether these systems usher in lasting success or merely temporary compliance. The true challenge lies not in merely defining these *Ideal Behavior*s but in crafting robust systems that consistently cultivate and reinforce them across the organization.

Process Intelligence plays a crucial role here by providing a structured approach to translating behavioral expectations into everyday practice. Through PQ, leaders can design and implement systems that nurture an environment of continual excellence that ensures every member of the organization not only meets but exceeds the standards set forth. This alignment between expectations and behaviors fuels a culture of integrity, innovation, and accountability while laying a solid foundation for enduring success.

By leveraging PQ to embed these behaviors deeply within organizational processes, we move beyond surface-level adherence to rules and regulations and foster a culture in which excellence is ingrained in the very fabric of our teams. This advancement is not just about achieving compliance, it is about motivating every individual to act with purpose and passion, united in their commitment to the organization's vision and goals. Through this transformation, we create a resilient, high-performing organization poised for long-term achievement and growth.

The Three Dimensions of Behavioral Excellence

The complexity of modern organizations requires an awareness of three important dimensions. First is cultural intelligence, which has become increasingly vital as organizations employ people from diverse backgrounds and traditions. These differences, while providing tremendous strength and competitive advantage, also create unique challenges in establishing consistent behaviors. Time perception varies significantly across cultures, with some viewing punctuality as arriving early while others consider being punctual as arriving after the stated time. Communication norms differ as well—from expectations about eye contact to personal space. Even decision-making approaches vary, with some cultures considering it disrespectful to challenge authority, while others expect there to be active debates.

Today's workplace often spans four distinct generations, and so the second dimension involves generational integration. Each generation brings unique perspectives and expectations to the table that are shaped by their experiences. Traditionalists value structure and clear authority while Baby Boomers seek involvement and recognition. Generation X prizes independence and results, and Millennials desire purpose and flexibility. Process Intelligence creates systems that honor these differences while maintaining consistent performance standards.

Communication style represents the third dimension. Some team members drive directly toward results while others focus on analyzing details. Some prioritize relationships while others thrive on energy and expression. High-functioning organizations create processes that enable effective communication across these varied styles while maintaining clear expectations and outcomes.

Low-Functioning vs. High-Functioning Behavior Systems

In organizations, the effectiveness of behavior systems can often distinguish between low-functioning and high-functioning environments. The dichotomy between these two types of behavior systems highlights significant differences in how expectations are set, how knowledge is managed, how onboarding is conducted, and how initiatives are iterated upon.

Low-Functioning Behavior Systems

In low-functioning environments, ambiguity reigns. Expectations are often unclear, which creates a breeding ground for conflict and confusion. Leaders may assume that team members understand their roles and responsibilities without verifying this understanding, leading to different interpretations of directives and subsequent misalignment. This lack of clarity results in a fragmented team environment where cohesive progress is challenging to achieve.

Moreover, critical skills and processes frequently reside as tribal knowledge, locked in the minds of individual employees. With the wave of Baby Boomer retirements—as many as 10,000 individuals leaving the workforce daily—organizations risk losing invaluable institutional knowledge that is overly dependent on specific personalities. This can cause a significant knowledge gap and disrupt the continuity of operations.

Additionally, onboarding in low-functioning systems is often personality-driven, relying heavily on IQ-based criteria alone. New hires are expected to "figure it out" because they possess the right credentials, which can create steep learning curves and inconsistent performance outcomes. This approach fails to provide a structured roadmap and can greatly hinder a newcomer's ability to adapt and thrive within the organization.

The presence of "dusty artifacts" characterizes low-functioning systems, in which failed initiatives pile up due to over-reliance on individual strengths due to a lack of systematic engagement processes. These remnants of past efforts breed cynicism about new programs as employees become jaded from having witnessed repeated failures.

High-Functioning Behavior Systems

In contrast, high-functioning environments cultivate the establishment of ideal behaviors through a clear and systematic process. They engage in ongoing discussions to define, document, and codify team behaviors, starting with fundamental questions about mutual expectations between leaders and team members. The resulting clarity fosters alignment and sets a solid foundation for collective success.

High-functioning organizations utilize a documented Business Process Handbook to systematically capture and transfer essential knowledge. This approach includes regular review cycles to ensure that content remains current and valuable and that it facilitates seamless assimilation of new members through structured onboarding programs. These systems ensure that critical knowledge is not lost and that new team members can fully integrate into the organization efficiently and effectively.

In terms of onboarding, high-functioning teams are system-driven, welcoming new hires and transfers with clear, established systems and expectations. The focus is on creating an inclusive environment that fosters collective success and allows new team members to quickly adapt and contribute to the organization's goals.

Furthermore, high-functioning teams often feature a robust iteration process with regular 90-day reviews that challenge the status quo by asking "So what?" about every process. This practice ensures processes remain relevant and continue to build on established foundations, promoting a culture of continuous improvement and innovation.

By shifting from low-functioning to high-functioning behavior systems, the effectiveness of organizations can be significantly enhanced while ensuring that every layer of the organization is aligned and optimized for sustainable success.

Leadership Traits in Behavioral Systems

The transformation to Process Intelligence fundamentally changes how leadership traits manifest in organizations. Humility shifts from a personal characteristic to a systematic approach for gathering feedback and driving improvement. Rather than depending primarily on charismatic personalities, organizations create clear processes that document expectations and facilitate continuous development.

Passion becomes channeled into creating and maintaining effective systems rather than on driving personal agendas. Leaders focus their energy on building sustainable processes that will outlast their tenure, rather than on becoming irreplaceable heroes. This approach ensures consistent execution regardless of who holds any particular position.

Stewardship transforms from personal responsibility to process accountability. Leaders become guardians of systems rather than problem-solvers, ensuring that knowledge transfers effectively and succession happens smoothly. This shift creates sustainable excellence that doesn't depend on individual capabilities.

Building Behavioral Sustainability

Leaders of high-functioning organizations recognize that sustainable behaviors require regular reinforcement through systematic processes. Every quarter, teams engage in structured reviews that examine not just what they're achieving, but how they're achieving it. These reviews move beyond simple compliance checks to deeply examine whether current behaviors align with organizational values and objectives.

Knowledge transfer becomes a continuous process rather than a crisis response whenever key employees leave. Organizations regularly document critical information and create clear pathways for developing new capabilities. This approach ensures that essential knowledge remains accessible even as team members change roles or leave the organization.

Cultural integration moves from an orientation event to an ongoing journey. New team members enter a systematic process that introduces them not just to what they need to do but how they need to do it. Regular touchpoints ensure consistent understanding and application of behavioral expectations across the organization.

Case Studies in Behavioral Transformation

Case Study 1: Manufacturing Excellence Through Improved Behavioral Systems

In a quest for consistent performance, a global manufacturer confronted a significant difference in performance across shifts, despite having identical equipment and processes. This company's journey towards transformation highlights the effectiveness of aligning behaviors systematically.

Incredibly, the manufacturing facility allowed disparate performance standards between shifts, resulting in inconsistent quality outcomes. There was heavy reliance on individual supervisors to maintain standards, which contributed to variability depending on who was overseeing a particular shift.

Furthermore, the lack of a structured knowledge transfer system meant that valuable information was not consistently shared or retained across teams.

To address these issues, the manufacturer developed a comprehensive procedural document outlining clear behavioral expectations for all employees, thereby establishing a unified standard for performance across shifts. They developed an onboarding process to ensure new hires were thoroughly acclimated to the company's standards and culture. They also implemented regular behavior reviews to continually assess compliance with these expectations, fostering accountability and continuous improvement. Additionally, robust knowledge transfer systems were developed to maintain and share essential information across the company.

The Results

The transformation yielded substantial results. The company experienced a 40% reduction in quality variations, significantly enhancing product consistency. Cross-shift consistency improved by 65%, demonstrating the effectiveness of behavioral alignment in standardizing operations. New hire ramp-up time was reduced by half, indicating that new team members were able to integrate and perform effectively much quicker than before. Lastly, there was an 85% increase in the number of documented processes, ensuring that critical knowledge was not only retained but accessible for ongoing use and improvement.

This case study underscores the impact that behavioral alignment can have on organizational performance, illustrating how clear expectations, consistent onboarding, and efficient knowledge management lead to enhanced operational excellence.

Creating Sustainable Behavioral Excellence

The transformation from personality-dependent to process-driven behaviors requires systematic approach:

Expectation Development Process

High-functioning organizations move beyond relying on assumptions by setting up clear processes to define and maintain behavioral standards, ensuring everyone operates with a consistent understanding of what is expected.

One of the more impactful exercises that CSI does with clients is to define and align team members on ideal behaviors and expectations

.

Leadership Team Alignment

At the core of this process is the achievement of cohesive alignment between leadership and team members. Leaders of organizations work to establish clearly defined mutual expectations in order to foster a more harmonious and productive work environment. They identify specific, observable behaviors that are both measurable and clear that promote consistency across the board. Expectations are regularly reviewed and refined to ensure they remain relevant and effective. Additionally, regular feedback mechanisms are implemented to facilitate open communication, thus allowing issues to be addressed swiftly and efficiently.

Knowledge Management

Knowledge management supports the sustainability of these processes through comprehensive documentation systems that thoroughly capture and maintain essential information. These systems are subject to regular updates, thereby ensuring they reflect the most current practices within the organization. Comprehensive knowledge transfer processes are established to enable smooth and uninterrupted sharing of information across teams to limit the occurrence of information silos. To ensure accountability and accuracy, responsibility for maintaining and updating this documentation is clearly assigned.

Onboarding Excellence

An excellent onboarding process is crucial for effectively integrating new team members. This process features a structured assimilation path, providing newcomers with a clear roadmap for them to successfully navigate their new roles. From the outset, new hires are provided with transparent expectations of the behaviors they are expected to adopt, aligned with the organization's standards.

Systematic skill development opportunities tailored to the specific roles of individuals help equip them to contribute effectively. Furthermore, regular progress reviews are conducted to monitor each new employee's development, offering continuous support and necessary adjustments to align with the organizational culture and expectations.

Cultural Integration

For organizations to achieve success, it's essential to move beyond mere documentation to create living behavioral systems seamlessly integrated into the company's culture.

Regular Assessment

A cornerstone of cultural integration is the commitment to regular assessment. Organizations conduct 90-day behavior reviews to evaluate how well team members are aligning with the expected behaviors. Clear measurement criteria are established to ensure that these reviews are objective and informative. Systematic feedback processes are utilized to provide constructive insights and to foster ongoing communication between team members and leadership. These assessments are part of continuous improvement mechanisms that encourage the organization to adapt and evolve in response to new challenges and opportunities.

Knowledge Evolution

Cultural integration also demands a dynamic approach to managing organizational knowledge. Regular content updates are crucial to keeping information current and applicable to today's needs. Systematic review processes ensure that every piece of content is evaluated for accuracy and relevance. Clear update protocols are established to maintain consistency and to prevent any gaps in knowledge. Finally, ongoing relevance checks are performed to guarantee that all documented practices and systems remain applicable and beneficial vis a vis the organization's objectives. This evolution of knowledge supports the creation of a robust, adaptable culture that is prepared to meet the demands of a changing environment

Conclusion

The Ideal Behavior Process represents the human foundation of Process Intelligence Leadership. Business Acumen provides direction, Execution drives action, and Communication ensures alignment, but behavior is what determines whether these systems create sustainable excellence or temporary compliance. Success requires moving beyond personality-dependent leadership to create systematic approaches to behavioral excellence. When organizations achieve this transformation, they build sustainable cultures that maintain high performance regardless of individual personalities or preferences.

The journey from low-functioning to high-functioning behavior isn't about better policies or stricter enforcement. It's about creating systematic processes that make ideal behaviors the natural way of working. When organizations achieve this transformation, they create sustainable excellence that transcends individual capabilities or personalities.

This sentiment is captured in a statement by Lynn A Bottone, VP Biotech Operations at Pfizer, "As I have progressed through my career, each role being more senior in nature, I have shared the Process Based Leadership® methodologies with my leadership teams to ensure we ground ourselves as a team. It takes work and continuous assessment of performance to transform good teams into great teams. And I can honestly say as I look back, the team I was leading when I first learned these methodologies turned out to be one of the best performing I have ever experienced. Hard work pays off!"

Pfizer

EPILOGUE
The Path Forward

As we reach the conclusion of our exploration into Process Intelligence, it's worth reflecting on the journey we've taken together. We began by challenging the conventional wisdom that effective leadership is solely a function of high intelligence and strong emotional intelligence. While these dimensions remain undeniably important, our investigation has revealed a critical third dimension that completes the leadership triangle: Process Intelligence.

This journey has taken us through the fundamental limitations of traditional leadership models and illuminated how even the most intelligent and emotionally astute leaders can struggle to create sustainable organizational success without the systems and processes that PQ provides. We've explored how organizations often fall into the trap of personality-dependent management—relying on the Three Ps of Position, Proximity, and Persuasion—and the inherent vulnerabilities this creates.

The Leadership Triangle: A New Paradigm

Our exploration has established that truly high-functioning leadership requires the integration of all three dimensions:

Intelligence Quotient provides the analytical foundation, the ability to understand complex problems, absorb information, and think strategically. It represents the "what" of leadership—what needs to be done, what challenges exist, and what opportunities are available. Organizations rightfully seek intelligent individuals who can comprehend the complexities of modern business and identify pathways to success.

Emotional Intelligence supplies the interpersonal capabilities to connect with others, understand human dynamics, and build relationships. It embodies the "who" of leadership—who needs to be engaged, who has valuable perspectives, and who requires different approaches when it comes to communication and motivation. The widespread recognition of EQ's importance has significantly advanced leadership development.

Process Intelligence delivers the systematic capabilities to design, implement, and sustain organizational systems that drive consistent results. It addresses the "how" of leadership—how to create sustainable excellence, how to scale success beyond individual heroics, and how to build organizations that thrive regardless of which personalities occupy key positions. This dimension has long been the missing link in leadership development, and it's the element that enables truly transformative leadership impact.

Together, these three dimensions create a powerful synergy. IQ without EQ produces brilliant strategies that teams struggle to embrace. EQ without IQ generates engaged teams working on the wrong priorities. IQ and EQ without PQ create temporary success that depends entirely on key individuals' continued presence and performance. Only the integration of all three dimensions creates sustainable organizational excellence.

The Four Components of Process Intelligence

Our journey has taken us deep into the four essential components of Process Intelligence, each addressing a critical aspect of organizational performance:

Business Acumen Process

The Business Acumen Process emphasizes strategic intelligence throughout the organization. It transforms the fundamental question "Are we winning or losing?" from a subjective assessment into a clear, metrics-driven evaluation that creates alignment at every level. Through structured scorecards, strategic frameworks, and systematic review processes, organizations move beyond the "thermometer" approach of passively reporting data to a "thermostat" model that actively drives performance improvement.

We've seen how organizations like Transform Manufacturing Corp successfully implemented this component, moving from scattered, conflicting metrics to a unified system that drove a 30% improvement in strategic alignment and a 25% reduction in decision-making cycle time. This transformation illustrates how PQ can turn business intelligence from an elite capability possessed by a few executives into an organizational asset that empowers everyone to contribute meaningfully to strategic success.

Execution Process

The Execution Process addresses the critical challenge of turning knowledge into action. It redefines execution from an emotional state of "feeling ownership" to a demonstrable set of actions that tangibly move the business forward. Through structured action registers, clear accountability frameworks, and consistent follow-up processes, this component ensures insights consistently translate into outcomes.

The transformation at REVLON demonstrated how this approach can dramatically improve organizational performance, leading to a 65% reduction in recurring issues and an 85% improvement in action completion rates. By connecting metrics to actions and actions to results, organizations create a culture of accountability that doesn't depend on heroic leadership intervention.

Communication Process

The Communication Process integrates Business Acumen and Execution into a coherent, effective dialogue system. It addresses the widespread problem of communication overload by focusing interactions on the critical question: "Did the time we just spend move our business forward?" Through structured meeting processes, standard agendas, and systematic effectiveness protocols, this component reclaims productive time and ensures that every conversation contributes to organizational success.

The six-hour meeting week framework provides a practical approach to streamlining communication while enhancing its impact. By integrating strategic review, operational review, and team development, organizations can create a rhythm of communication that drives alignment and action without overwhelming calendars or exhausting participants.

Ideal Behavior Process

The Ideal Behavior Process represents the human foundation of Process Intelligence Leadership. It addresses the essential question: "Are we living up to, or falling short of, our ideal behaviors?" By defining, documenting, and reinforcing expectations, this component ensures that work aligns with organizational values and objectives.

Case studies from manufacturing and healthcare demonstrate how this approach can significantly reduce performance variations and enhance consistency across teams and locations. Organizations create sustainable excellence that transcends individual leaders or personalities by moving beyond personality-dependent models of cultural integration to systematic processes for knowledge management, onboarding, and behavioral reinforcement.

The Transformation Challenge

Throughout our exploration, we've acknowledged that the journey to Process Intelligence Leadership isn't simple or straightforward. Organizations face significant challenges in making this transformation, including:

Cultural Resistance: The shift from personality-driven to process-driven leadership often meets resistance from those who have succeeded under the traditional model. Leaders who have risen through the ranks based on their IQ and EQ may feel threatened by a system that seems to diminish the importance of these capabilities. Overcoming this resistance requires demonstrating that PQ doesn't replace IQ and EQ but amplifies their impact and creates sustainability.

The Urgency Trap: The constant pressure of daily operations can make it difficult for organizations to invest in building systematic processes. The irony is that this urgency is often a symptom of the very problem PQ addresses—without effective systems, organizations remain trapped in firefighting mode, unable to create the space for strategic improvement.

Breaking this cycle requires courage and discipline to prioritize process development even amid operational demands.

Implementation Complexity: Building robust systems requires specialized knowledge and significant effort. Many organizations begin with enthusiasm but struggle to maintain momentum when confronted with the detailed work of designing, implementing, and refining processes. Success requires both committed leadership and practical implementation support.

Sustainability Challenges: Even organizations that successfully implement process improvements often struggle to maintain them over time. Without systematic reinforcement mechanisms, processes tend to degrade as new priorities emerge, leadership changes, or external pressures intensify. Creating truly sustainable Process Intelligence requires building self-reinforcing systems that include regular review, refinement, and renewal.

Despite these challenges, the case studies we've examined demonstrate that successful transformation is not only possible but delivers profound benefits. Organizations that effectively integrate PQ into their leadership model experience enhanced performance, reduced leader stress, improved succession capabilities, and sustainable excellence that transcends individual contributions.

The Personal Journey

While our focus has been on organizational systems, it's important to recognize that Process Intelligence also represents a personal journey for leaders at all levels. This journey involves several key shifts in thinking and behavior:

From Hero to Architect: Many leaders derive their identity and satisfaction from being the indispensable problem-solver, the hero who saves the day through personal intervention. Process Intelligence requires redefining success as creating systems where such heroics are rarely necessary. This shift can be challenging but liberating, as leaders discover the deeper impact and legacy of building sustainable systems.

From Controller to Enabler: Traditional leadership often emphasizes control, ensuring that teams follow directions and meet expectations through close supervision and intervention. Process Intelligence Leadership focuses instead on enabling teams through clear processes that provide guidance and autonomy. This shift creates more scalable leadership and more engaged teams.

From Knowing to Learning: Leaders can no longer rely solely on their accumulated knowledge and experience in rapidly changing environments. Process Intelligence creates systems for organizational learning, enabling leaders to absorb new insights and adapt strategies accordingly continuously. This shift from static knowledge to dynamic learning is essential for sustainable success.

From Individual to Collective Leadership: Perhaps most fundamentally, Process Intelligence requires moving beyond the model of the singular heroic leader to create collective leadership capability distributed throughout the organization. This shift doesn't diminish the importance of individual leaders but amplifies their impact by creating systems that enable everyone to contribute at their highest level.

As you reflect on your leadership journey, consider where you fall on these continua and what shifts might enhance your effectiveness and legacy. The workbook exercises provided throughout this book offer practical tools for this self-assessment and development process.

Building Your PQ Development Plan

As we conclude our exploration, I encourage you to develop a specific plan for enhancing Process Intelligence in your leadership and organization. This plan should address both personal development and organizational implementation:

Personal PQ Development: Assess your current strengths and opportunities in each component of Process Intelligence. Identify specific skills you must develop to design, implement, and sustain effective systems. Seek opportunities to learn from others who excel in this dimension and practice these capabilities in your leadership role.

Team PQ Building: Work with your direct team to build Process Intelligence capabilities collectively. Use the assessment tools provided to identify improvement opportunities and engage the team in designing and implementing enhanced processes. Celebrate progress and recognize contributions to building a more systematic approach.

Organizational PQ Implementation: Advocate for Process Intelligence as a strategic priority within your organization. Share this book's concepts and case studies with peers and leaders to build understanding and commitment. Work to integrate PQ development into leadership training, succession planning, and organizational improvement initiatives.

Remember that this journey is iterative and ongoing. Start with manageable initiatives demonstrating Process Intelligence's value, then build on these successes to create broader organizational impact. Document your approach and results to create a case for continued investment in this dimension of leadership development.

The Future of Leadership

As we look to the future, several trends make Process Intelligence increasingly critical for organizational success:

Accelerating Change: Technological, market and social change continues to accelerate, creating an environment where rigid, personality-dependent leadership models cannot adapt quickly enough. Process Intelligence provides the flexibility to navigate this rapidly evolving landscape.

Demographic Shifts: The ongoing retirement of Baby Boomers, combined with changing workforce expectations among younger generations, creates both a knowledge transfer crisis and a leadership approach mismatch. Process Intelligence addresses both challenges by systematically preserving essential knowledge and creating leadership systems that align with emerging workforce preferences for autonomy, purpose, and growth.

Remote and Hybrid Work: The dramatic shift toward distributed work arrangements demands new approaches to leadership that don't rely on physical proximity or personal charisma. Process Intelligence provides structured systems to maintain consistency, clarity, and accountability across dispersed teams.

Complexity Management: Organizations face increasingly complex challenges that transcend individual capabilities, requiring collaborative approaches and systematic solutions.

Process Intelligence creates the frameworks for effectively addressing this complexity through collective intelligence and coordinated action.

Organizations that develop strong Process Intelligence will be better positioned to navigate these challenges successfully. By creating systems that enable consistent execution, continuous learning, and sustainable adaptation, they will build competitive advantages that transcend individual talents or market fluctuations.

Leaving a Leadership Legacy

We began this journey with a fundamental question: Why do some leaders leave an indelible mark on their organizations while others, once gone, appear to have never been there at all? The answer lies largely in Process Intelligence—the ability to create systems and processes that outlive one's tenure and continue to drive organizational success.

Leaders who rely solely on IQ and EQ may achieve impressive results during their time at the helm, but these results often fade quickly after their departure. The dependency on their specific capabilities creates a vacuum that new leaders struggle to fill, often leading to performance declines, strategic shifts, and cultural erosion.

In contrast, leaders who develop strong Process Intelligence leave a tangible legacy that continues to shape organizational performance long after they've moved on. The systems they build—for strategic clarity, execution discipline, effective communication, and behavioral excellence—become part of the organization's DNA, providing a foundation for sustained success regardless of who holds leadership positions.

This enduring impact represents the true measure of leadership effectiveness. Beyond quarterly results or annual bonuses, beyond recognition or status, the ability to build something that outlasts your presence defines a genuine leadership legacy. Process Intelligence is the key to creating this lasting impact.

A Call to Action

As we conclude this exploration of Process Intelligence Leadership, we invite you to consider how these concepts apply to your leadership journey and organizational context. Whether you're a seasoned executive, a midlevel manager, a frontline supervisor, or an aspiring leader, the principles of Process Intelligence offer a pathway to greater impact and more sustainable success.

Begin by assessing your current approach to leadership. How dependent is your team's success on your personal intervention? What would happen if you were suddenly unavailable for an extended period? Would systems continue to function effectively, or would performance rapidly deteriorate? Honest answers to these questions can reveal opportunities to enhance Process Intelligence.

Next, consider starting with one component of PQ where you see the greatest opportunity for improvement. Perhaps your organization needs a clearer Business Acumen Process to align and enable a better understanding of performance. Maybe the Execution Process requires strengthening to ensure consistent follow-through on commitments. Perhaps the Communication Process needs restructuring to reclaim time and to enhance impact. Or maybe the Ideal Behavior Process requires attention to create more consistent expectations and knowledge transfer.

Begin with manageable initiatives demonstrating the value of a more systematic approach. Document your baseline performance and track improvements to build the case for broader implementation. Share your experiences with colleagues to expand the impact beyond your immediate area of responsibility.

Remember that Process Intelligence isn't about creating rigid bureaucracy or eliminating the human element from leadership. On the contrary, it's about creating the foundation that allows intellectual brilliance and emotional connection to achieve their full potential. It's about building organizations where everyone can contribute at their highest level without being limited by dysfunction, confusion, or inconsistency.

The journey to Process Intelligence is challenging but profoundly rewarding. It offers the opportunity to build something truly lasting. This organization performs excellently not because of extraordinary individual heroics but because of extraordinary systems that bring out the best in ordinary people daily.

We invite you to join me on this journey. Together, we can redefine leadership effectiveness and create organizations that stand the test of time, leaving a legacy that truly matters.

The future belongs to leaders who master IQ, EQ, and PQ. Will you be among them?

Shane Yount

Rob Kornblum

ABOUT THE AUTHORS

Meet Shane Yount

Shane A. Yount is a nationally recognized thought leader, author, and Chairman & Founder of Competitive Solutions, Inc., (CSI) an international Business Transformation consulting firm headquartered in Raleigh, NC. CSI pioneered the acclaimed organizational development system known as Process Based Leadership®, a business transformation methodology designed to create sustainable cultures of clarity, connectivity, and consistency through the use of Non-Negotiable Business Processes.

Shane began his career with Perdue Farms, Inc. Having performed such roles as Front Line Supervisor, Operations Manager, Quality Manager, Director of Human Resources, and Corporate Continuous Improvement Champion, Shane brings extensive experience in every aspect of organizational dynamics. His *"Real World"* process-driven approach to creating and sustaining high performance has led leaders across the world to embrace the Process Based Leadership® methodology as a core operating system to scale and sustain operational excellence. Since 1991 he has led the offices of Competitive Solutions, Inc. (CSI), personally working with such organizations as Pfizer, 3M, Colgate-Palmolive, Revlon, Impossible Foods, the US Army, and countless others. His three books, *Buried Alive: Digging out of the Management Dumpster, Leaving Your Leadership Legacy* and *Leading Your Business Forward: Aligning Goals, People, and Systems for Sustainable Success* are required reading in many organizations.

Shane has been married for 30 years to his wife Stephanie. They have two sons, Parker and Will and a new daughter-in-law, Rachel. Shane and his family have deep roots in North Carolina and in his free time can often be found on his boat off the southern coast of NC. Outside of CSI, Shane loves to snow ski, run competitively, travel, and cheer on his Carolina Hurricanes and UNC Tar Heels.

Meet Rob Kornblum

Rob Kornblum has more than 25 years of experience as a growth company executive, venture capitalist, and entrepreneur. He is currently President & CEO of Competitive Solutions, Inc. (CSI), an international Business Transformation consulting firm.

He was previously Portfolio Fund Manager American Family Insurance Institute, a social impact venture capital fund, where he led multiple investments and was on numerous Boards of Directors. Rob was previously a senior executive at several high-growth public and private technology and services companies. Rob held senior roles at Avention, Inc (acquired by Dun & Bradstreet), Lifecare (a private benefits company), and Monster Worldwide, where he led over $100M of contract value from media partnerships. He was also VP/GM at Bullhorn, a high-growth SaaS company.

He was previously a Principal at Austin Ventures, Managing Director at ANGLE Technology, and head of alliances at Manugistics.

Rob has an undergraduate degree from Dartmouth College, an MBA from the Kellogg School of Management at Northwestern University, and is a Kauffman Fellow.

He is a best-selling author (Never Too Late to Startup and Entrepreneur Rocket Fuel), speaker, blogger, and entrepreneur coach. He speaks regularly at Boston University, Harvard Business School, and mentors at MassChallenge and Babson College.

Rob has been married for 29 years to his wife Suzie. Rob lives in the Boston area and is a passionate Boston sports fan. In his spare time, Rob likes to cook, garden, and travel.